DIVERTICULITIS COOKBOOK

QUICK & EASY CLEAR LIQUID, LOW RESIDUE, & HIGH FIBER RECIPES WITH 12-WEEK MEAL PLAN TO NATURALLY PREVENT FLARE-UPS, ENJOY PAIN-FREE FOODS AND BOOST YOUR DIGESTIVE SYSTEM

© COPYRIGHT 2021 - ALL RIGHTS RESERVED.

This document is geared towards providing exact and reliable information in regard to the topic and issue covered.

- From a Declaration of Principles which was accepted and approved equally by a Committee of the American Bar Association and a Committee of Publishers and Associations.

In no way is it legal to reproduce, duplicate, or transmit any part of this document in either electronic means or in printed format. All rights reserved.

The information provided herein is stated to be truthful and consistent, in that any liability, in terms of inattention or otherwise, by any usage or abuse of any policies, processes, or directions contained within is the solitary and utter responsibility of the recipient reader. Under no circumstances will any legal responsibility or blame be held against the publisher for any reparation, damages, or monetary loss due to the information herein, either directly or indirectly.

Respective authors own all copyrights not held by the publisher.

The information herein is offered for informational purposes solely and is universal as so. The presentation of the information is without contract or any type of guarantee assurance.

The trademarks that are used are without any consent, and the publication of the trademark is without permission or backing by the trademark owner. All trademarks and brands within this book are for clarifying purposes only and are owned by the owners themselves, not affiliated with this document.

Table of Contents

INTRODUCTION.................................13

CHAPTER 1: UNDERSTANDING DIVERTICULAR DISEASE -...................................15

CHAPTER 2: MASTER THE 3 PHASES OF NUTRITION...................................18

CHAPTERT 3: SHOPPING LIST 20

CHAPTER 4: CLEAR FLUIDS..................24

1. Strawberry Apple Juice..........................25
2. Fall Energizer Juice................................25
3. Mushroom, Cauliflower and Cabbage Broth....25
4. Ginger, Mushroom and Cauliflower Broth........26
5. Fish Broth..26
6. Clear Pumpkin Broth.............................26
7. Pork Stock...27
8. Slow Cooker Pork Bone Broth...............27
9. Homemade No Pulp Orange Juice.......27
10. Apple Orange Juice 28
11. Pineapple Mint Juice 28
12. Homey Clear Chicken Broth...............29
13. Asian Inspired Wonton Broth.............29
14 Oxtail Bone Broth.................................29
15. Beef Bone Broth..................................30
16. Indian Inspired Vegetable stock.........30

17. ThreeIngredien..31
Sugar-Free Gelatin...31
18. Cranberry Kombucha Jell-O.......................31
19. Strawberry Gummies..................................31
20. Fruity Jell-O Stars.......................................31
21. Plum and Nectarine Gelatin Pudding.........32
22. Homemade Lemon Gelatin........................32
23. Sour Blueberry Gummies...........................32
24 Sugar-Free Cinnamon Jelly........................33
25. Chicken Vegetable Soup............................33
26. Carrot Ginger Soup....................................33
27. Turkey Sweet Potato Hash.........................34
28. Chicken Tenders with Honey Mustard Sauce..34
29. Chicken Breasts with Cabbage and Mushrooms..35
30. Duck with Bok Choy..................................35
31. Beef with Mushroom and Broccoli............35
32. Beef with Zucchini Noodles......................36
33. Spiced Ground Beef..................................36
34. Ground Beef with Veggies.........................37
35. Gala Apple Flavored Ice Cubes.................38
36. Kale Flavored Ice Cubes............................38
37. Cranberry Flavored Ice Cubes...................38
38. Banana Ice Cubes......................................38
39. Elderberry Gummies..................................39
40. Blackberry-Rose Ice Pops..........................39
41. Frozen Strawberry-Peach Pops..................39
42. Honey Lemonade Popsicles......................40
43. Orange Strawberry Popsicles....................40
44. Melon Basil Moscow Mule Popsicles.........40
45. Honeydew Mint Homemade Popsicles......41

CHAPTER 5: LOW RESIDUALS.............42

46. Breakfast Cereal..................................43
47. Sweet Potato Hash with Sausage and Spinach..43
48. Cajun Omelet.....................................43
48. Strawberry Cashew Chia Pudding................43
50. Peanut Butter Banana Oatmeal....................44
51. Overnight Peach Oatmeal........................44
52. Mediterranean Salmon and Potato Salad....44
53. Pea Tuna Salad...................................45
54. Carrot and Turkey Soup.........................45
55. Creamy Pumpkin Soup............................45
56 Chicken Pea Soup.................................46
57. Garden Veggies Quiche..........................46
58. Fluffy Pumpkin Pancakes........................46
59. Super-Tasty Chicken Muffins...................47
60. Classic Zucchini Bread.........................47
61. Greek Inspired Cucumber Salad.................48
62. Light Veggie Salad.............................48
63. Eastern European Soup..........................48
64. Citrus Glazed Carrots..........................49
65. Spring Flavored Pasta..........................49
66. Gluten-Free Curry..............................49
67. Almond Peanut Butter Fudge.....................50
68. Quick Cocoa Mousse.............................50
69. Cinnamon Pear Chips............................51
70. Chocolate Yogurt Cream & Roasted Bananas 51
71. Coconut Celery Smoothie........................51
72. Apple Spinach Smoothie.........................52
73. Banana Cocoa Cream.............................48
74. Homemade Pumpkin Pie...........................52
75. Zero Sugar Pumpkin Pie.........................53
76. Orange Curd....................................53

77. Instant Pot Pear Crumble.................53
78. Chicken Cutlets...................54
79. Slow Cooker Salsa Turkey...............54
80. Sriracha Lime Chicken and Apple Salad......55
81. Pan-Seared Scallops with Lemon-Ginger Vinaigrette...................55
82. Roasted Salmon and Asparagus..............56
83. Cod with Ginger and Black Beans...........56
84. Halibut Curry......................56
85. Chicken Cacciatore..................57
86. Chicken and Bell Pepper Saute'.............57
87. Chicken Salad Sandwiches................57
88. Rosemary Chicken....................58
89. Papaya-Mango Smoothie................59
90. Cantaloupe Smoothie..................59
91. Cantaloupe-Mix Smoothie...............59
92. Applesauce-Avocado Smoothie............59
93. Pina Colada Smoothie.................56
94. Diced Fruits......................60
95. Applesauce........................60
96. Avocado Dip......................61
97. Homemade Hummus..................61
98. Tofu............................61

CHAPTER 6: HIGH-FIBER DIET..............63

99. Pear Turkey Pita....................64
100. Overnight Oats....................64
101. Veggie Scramble...................64
102. Turkey and Avocado Pitas.............64
103. Grilled Vegetable Sandwich............65
104. Spinach and Ham Pizza...............65
105. Fruit Bowl......................65
106. Easy Tofu & Beans..................66

107. Couscous with Dates..................66
108. Bean & Vegetable Pasta..............66
109. Pork and Penne Pasta................67
110. Chicken and Quinoa Pita.............67
111. Chicken and Asparagus Pasta.........68
112. Turkey Florentine...................68
113. Chicken Lettuce Wraps...............69
114. Couscous with Turkey................69
115. Easy Turkey Chili...................69
116. Ham, Bean and Cabbage Stew..........70
117. Grilled Fish Tacos..................70
118. Pasta with Turkey and Olives........71
119. Rice Bowl with Shrimp and Peas......71
120. Ricotta & Cannellini Salad..........72
121. Bean and Tomato Salad...............72
122. String bean Potato Salad............72
123. Cucumber Peach Salad................73
124. Strawberry & Apple Salad............73
125. Bean and Couscous Salad.............73
126. Asian Chicken Salad.................73
127. Almond Salad........................74
128. Vegetarian Nuttolene Salad..........74
129. Nutty Green Salad...................74
130. One-Pot Dinner Soup.................75
131. 3-Beans Soup.......................76
132. Heavenly Tasty Stew.................76
133. Thanksgiving Dinner Chili...........77
134. Meatless Monday Chili...............77
135. Beans Trio Chili....................78
136. Staple Vegan Curry..................78
137. Fragrant Vegetarian Curry...........79
138. Omega-3 Rich Dinner Meal............79
139. Weekend Dinner Casserole............80

140. Family Dinner Pilaf..................................81
141. Whole-wheat–Chocolate Chip Cookies........81
142. Good-for-You Chocolate Chip Cookies........81
143. Oat and Wheat Cookies.................................82
144. Oatmeal Spice Cookies..................................82
145. Trail Mix Cookies...83
146. White Chocolate-Cranberry Cookies...........83
147. Oatmeal Sunflower Bread............................84
148. Maple Oatmeal Bread...................................84
149. German Dark Bread......................................84
150. Onion and Garlic Wheat Bread....................85

CHAPTER 7: MENTAL APPROACH TO THE DISORDER, DEVELOPING RESILIENCE 86

CHAPTER 8: EMOTIONAL RESILIENCE AND MEDITATIONEXCERCISES................................86

CHAPTER 9: HOW TO MANAGE TROUBLESOME SYMPTOMS WITH MEDITATIONS, MINDFULNESS, YOGA, EXERCISES ACCORDING TO YOUR PERSONALITY........................98

ILLUSTRATION OF YOGA TECHNIQUES, MINDFULNESS, AND CONCEPTS ON HOW TO INCREASE RESILIENCE 101

CONCLUSION 104

REFERENCES..106

FOOD JOURNAL..106

INTRODUCTION

Diverticulitis is a condition in which pouches or pockets form on the wall of your colon, usually on the left-hand side of the large intestine. These pouches are known as diverticula. The condition is caused by an infection with bacteria called "Clostridium difficile" (C diff). C diff usually spreads when bowel movements are not properly eliminated, when stool becomes too watery, or when stools contain mucous. Other risk factors include diarrhea and antibiotic use. Symptoms of diverticulitis include cramping, fever, diarrhea, nausea, and vomiting.

The diet for diverticulitis should be a clear liquid diet for the first 72 hours after your attack. You should then slowly reintroduce solid foods until your symptoms have resolved.

It is important to know that the following diet helps prevent future attacks of diverticulitis by reducing toxins in your colon. Your colon needs enough bacteria to do this job effectively. Adding more than 15 grams of dietary fiber a day to your diet, however, may increase your risk of diverticulitis.

Here are some other guidelines to follow while you are seeking medical treatment for your diverticulitis:

These dietary changes will not cure your diverticulitis. However, you should notice an improvement within three to four weeks after making these diet changes. If you can maintain these diet changes, you will probably be able to prevent future attacks of diverticulitis. The best results occur when your total fiber intake remains below 15 g per day. Be sure to discuss this with your physician before making any major changes in the diet.

HERE'S WHAT YOU NEED TO KNOW ABOUT SPECIFIC FOODS AND DRINKS:

- Avoid high-fiber foods such as whole grains, nuts, seeds, beans, and popcorn. Instead, keep to a low-fiber diet by avoiding fruits, vegetables, and high-fiber foods.
- For dairy products, choose skim milk or nonfat, vegetarian milk alternatives such as soy milk, rice milk, or almond milk. Cottage cheeses are an exception because they are generally made with whole milk.
- Choose fresh fruits and vegetables rather than canned. Canned items are generally made with added preservatives to prevent spoilage.
- Only drink water when thirsty, not when bloated from gas production. Keep in mind that some added sugars may cause gas production in your digestive system.
- Avoid caffeinated drinks, which can cause a sharp rise in carbon dioxide production.
- Emphasize minimally processed, low-sugar foods such as lean meat, fish, and poultry.
- Consider a natural omega-3 fatty acid supplement if you take antibiotics because they may interfere with the absorption of the antibiotic. Also, avoid high-fiber diets for several weeks before starting other medications to make sure your body is not fighting off the other medication at the same time you are battling your diverticulitis.

CHAPTER 1
UNDERSTANDING DIVERTICULAR DISEASE

Diverticular disease (DD) is the inflammation of the wall of a pouch-like structure in the large intestine called a diverticulum. DD usually occurs when this pouch's natural barriers (i.e., muscularis mucosa) are disrupted by reduced blood supply or bacterial invasion. This weakening allows bacteria to enter the gut wall and cause inflammation with serious consequences for digestion, bowel function, and even life itself.

Diverticula may occur in the wall of any part of the large intestine but are most common in the last three or four parts of the colon. The diverticular disease usually begins within a diverticulum, but this may also start in a small area immediately adjacent to a diverticulum or along a patchy portion of the colonic wall that is susceptible to bulging outwards because it has not been completely covered by the usual outpouching. In some cases, especially when many diverticula have already formed, inflammation from one diverticulum can spread to neighboring pouches and cause them to become inflamed as well.

CAUSES OF THE PROBLEM

Diverticula can form when certain parts of the colon become blocked, which causes bacteria to collect in the pouch. These bacteria multiply, and when they feed on the food they produce gas (known as gas diarrhea) which makes the pouch swell up.

Diverticulosis, in general, occurs when small pockets in the large intestine (colon) become weak and stretchy enough to allow bacteria like E. coli bacteria, Clostridium difficile, H. pylori, or gluten to enter the wall through tiny holes called fistulas. These bacteria grow in the pouch and multiply.

DD IS MOST COMMONLY CAUSED BY A COMBINATION OF TWO OR MORE OF THE FOLLOWING:

- Surgical operations are the most common cause of diverticular disease, especially operations related to bowel surgery—the most common surgical operations are colorectal surgery, surgery for cancer, diverticulitis, perforation of anus after anal fissure, post-operative stress reaction, Hirschsprung's disease, Crohn's disease.
- Changes in diet/lifestyle/lifestyle change, obesity.
- Missing toilet or stool on time.
- Chronic constipation.
- Men with DD seem to face a higher risk of developing Crohn's disease.
- A high-fat diet.
- Low dietary fiber.
- Inactivity.
- Incomplete evacuation of stool.
- Age.
- Family history.
-

All these causes lead to an accumulation of bacteria in the intestine wall, which in turn causes inflammation and swelling in the inflamed area.

In most cases, people who have had surgery are not able to return to their previous lifestyle for some time. The resulting low-fiber diet without regular physical exercise means that their bowels become inactive and do not work properly.

FUNDAMENTAL INDICATIONS

1. The patient should be fully aware of the fact that DD does not belong to the acute abdomen but still requires urgent treatment because of its life-threatening complications.
2. The physician should immediately rule out serious conditions that cause abdominal pain or dyspepsia, such as appendicitis, pancreatitis, cholecystitis, hepatitis, and gastrointestinal bleeding.
3. Bowel movement should be checked at first to determine whether it is due to diarrhea or constipation.
4. The next step is to check the type of stool because it may be accompanied by blood admixed with stools or other abnormalities.
5. The red flag sign is abdominal pain after eating because this may indicate colonic narrowing, hemorrhage, or toxic colitis.
6. Checking if the patient has had anemia, lymphoma (thymoma), and inflammatory bowel disease.
7. Checking if the patient has had recent operations due to a tumor or diverticulitis.
8. To determine the subtype of DD (i.e., diverticular bleeding, acute abdomen).
9. To find the amount of bowel movements.
10. To decide whether the problem is transient or chronic, i.e., how long it will take to heal.

PROGNOSIS

The prognosis depends on the severity of complications and treatment. If the diverticula burst without causing intestinal bleeding, there is a good chance for recovery, but if either large segments of the intestine or perforation occurs, then the chances are very low for recovery. DD is diagnosed in between 1-2% of all people admitted to hospital with abdominal pain, though it may be more common in older people and in patients with poor nutritional status.

order to make an accurate diagnosis. If the diverticular disease is strongly suspected, the patient may undergo additional examinations, such as blood tests, x-rays, and colonoscopy.

SYMPTOMS

The main symptom of diverticular disease is intermittent abdominal pain that comes on suddenly, lasts for up to 24 hours, and subsides within 24 hours. The pain may be mild or severe, and milder pain may last for several weeks. Other symptoms include:

- Vomiting, nausea, or diarrhea.
- Pain in the right lower quadrant.
- Pain in the shoulder blades tingling sensation.
- Difficulty passing urine bloody tarry stools (feces); pain in the abdomen may be felt by pressure on the abdomen, which leads to a feeling of fullness. Difficulty with defecation is called having tenesmus; tenesmus can be made worse by physical activity, stress, or anxiety.

DIVERTICULITIS VS. DIVERTICULOSIS

Even though they have similar symptoms, the two conditions are different and need to be distinguished:

1. Most of the time, diverticulitis and diverticular disease occur in the same location (diverticulitis). If diverticulitis is present, it usually follows either an acute attack of appendicitis or bowel obstruction. The problem also occasionally results from an operation or other medical treatment such as radiation therapy to the abdomen (radiation proctitis). The diverticular disease usually occurs spontaneously without any preceding infection.
2. Often, diverticular disease is asymptomatic. In such cases, it can be detected by colonoscopy or CT, or MRI.
3. If the diverticula protrudes from the colon wall, you can call it diverticulosis. Most of the time, the diverticulum is flat and does not cause any symptoms.

DIAGNOSIS

Most often, there are no specific signs to support a diagnosis of diverticular disease. The disease must therefore be diagnosed based on anamnesis, clinical examination, and laboratory data. Symptoms are similar to other diseases that cause abdominal pain, resulting in subsequent visits to the doctor conducting various additional examinations until there is a correct diagnosis. A doctor must be familiar with the disease in

CHAPTER 2
MASTER THE 3 PHASES OF NUTRITION

WHAT TO EAT IN THE 3 PHASES OF THE DIET?

The following foods are suggested for each stage:
- Phase 1: Clear liquids and light snacks without dairy or red meat.
- Phase 2: Regular food, but excluding all dairy and red meat.
- Phase 3: Full food intake after consultation with your doctor.

These recommendations may vary depending on the severity of your condition and your specific needs as an individual. The three-stage diet is only meant as a general guideline for those who have already completed the first two stages. The specifics will be determined by your individual case as well as any medications that you're taking during this time.

EXPLANATION OF THE 3 STAGES OF THE DIET

If you've suffered from diverticulitis, you know how unpleasant it can be. This infection of the colon can result in painful diarrhea, cramping, and even hemorrhoids. If left untreated, the condition can quickly worsen to the point that it becomes life-threatening.

That's why we've put together this quick guide on diverticulitis diets to help sufferers with their treatment by outlining three different stages of this restrictive diet plan: Stage 1 includes clear liquids and light snacks; Stage 2 allows for regular foods but no dairy or red meat; and finally stage 3 with full food intake after consultation with your doctor.

STAGE 1

This is the easiest stage of the Diverticulitis diet. Since you're only able to eat clear liquids and light snacks, many patients can get back to normal eating after just a couple of days. If you're suffering from diarrhea, it's best to avoid making too many intense transitions from solids to liquids or vice versa, as this can aggravate your condition. Your body simply needs time to adjust between those two extremes.

STAGE 2

This begins at about six weeks after your doctors removed all pieces of the inflamed bowel with sedation and will continue until you have been symptom-free for five days at a time. At this time, your doctor may recommend that you begin taking probiotics.

STAGE 3

You are now ready to go back to a regular diet after consulting with your doctor. While it's still recommended that you eat small meals throughout the day, there are no longer any restrictions on dairy or red meat intake. The only difference between this stage and being completely symptom-free is that you may have to wait for a few days before returning to your normal diet if you experience bloating or gas.

It's important to note that each diverticulitis diet plan will be different for each individual patient. Although Stage 1 is the most restrictive (and, therefore, the easiest to complete), your specific case will dictate how quickly you can return to a normal diet.

Here are some additional tips that you should keep in mind while completing this diet plan:

1. Eat small meals throughout the day; this will give your body more time to digest (this is ideal for preventing bloating and gas). This same rule applies when eating any type of food. Do not stuff yourself in one sitting; rather, try to eat the recommended number of bite-sized portions throughout each day. If you're not sure about how many bites are considered a serving, just check with your healthcare provider or dietician.

2. Do not eat any raw fruits or vegetables; these foods can irritate your gut and increase your symptoms. If they must be eaten, make sure that they're very well-cooked and soft. Try steaming them instead of boiling them. Also, avoid hot beverages, as these can also irritate your colon.

3. Dairy products such as milk and yogurt are the only sources of calcium in most diets; however, they should be avoided here because they may aggravate symptoms during this stage of the diverticulitis diet. Try switching to an alternative high-calcium food such as soy milk or almond milk and taking a calcium supplement along with regular multivitamins for added protection. Some patients find that taking calcium lactate capsules is effective in reducing symptoms.

4. Avoid sugar and starches; if you need to eat something sweet, opt for fruit or starchy vegetables instead. Cutting down on refined carbohydrates can help to prevent bloating and gas problems. This is also a good time to introduce more protein into your diet.

5. Eat more fiber-rich foods such as fruits, vegetables, beans, lentils, nuts, seeds, and whole grains. You can also try taking high-fiber probiotics along with high-fiber foods to boost your digestive enzymes and help heal the irritated intestinal lining.

CHAPTER 3
SHOPPING LIST

FRUITS

- Apple Sauce
- Apples
- Apricots
- Bananas
- Dates
- Mangoes
- Oranges
- Peaches
- Prunes

JUICES

- Apple Juice
- Lemon Juice
- Lime Juice
- Orange Juice
- Cranberry Juice

VEGETABLES

- Alfalfa Sprouts
- Artichoke Hearts
- Asparagus
- Avocados
- Black Olives
- Broccoli
- Butternut Squash
- Cabbage
- Carrots
- Cauliflower
- Celery
- Eggplants
- Garlic
- Green Bell Peppers (seedless)
- Green Olives
- Green Onions
- Leeks
- Mushrooms
- Lettuce
- Olives
- Onions
- Peas (frozen, cooked)
- Pimento
- Red Bell Peppers (seedless)
- Russet Potatoes
- Shallots
- Spinach
- Sugar Snap Peas
- Summer Squash
- Yellow Peppers (seedless)
- Tomatoes (seedless)
- Water chestnuts
- Zucchini
- Sweet Yams

BEANS & PEAS

- Black Beans
- Butter Beans
- Cannellini Beans
- Garbanzo Beans
- Canned Kidney Beans
- Lentils
- Canned Lima Beans
- Canned Navy Beans
- Canned Red Beans

GRAINS, BREAD & OTHER STARCHES

- All-Bran Cereal
- Barley
- Brown Rice
- Fiber One Cereal
- Long Grain Rice
- Oat Bran
- Rolled Oats

- Whole Wheat Tortellini
- Whole Wheat Flour
- Whole Wheat Pasta
- Whole Wheat Pita
- Whole Wheat Tortillas
- Whole Wheat Bread

MEATS

- Crab Meat, Cooked
- Ground Chicken, Lean
- Ground Turkey, Lean
- Lean Ham
- Shrimp, large, peeled
- Canned Tuna Fish in water
- Turkey Breast
- Chicken Breast

DAIRY

- Cheddar Cheese (low-fat)
- Cottage Cheese (low-fat)
- Cream Cheese (low-fat)
- Feta Cheese
- Monterrey Jack Cheese (low-fat)
- Parmesan Cheese
- Eggs
- Half-and-half cream
- Milk, low-fat
- Yogurt, low-fat
- Spices, Herbs & Oils
- Baking Powder
- Basil (fresh or dried)
- Canola Oil
- Cilantro (fresh)
- Cinnamon powder
- Cumin
- Curry Powder
- Dill, (fresh or dried)

- Italian Seasoning
- Nutmeg
- Olive Oil
- Oregano, (fresh and dried)
- Italian parsley (fresh)
- Sage (fresh)
- Tarragon (fresh)
- Thyme (fresh and dried)
- Vanilla

CONDIMENTS

- Vegetable Stock
- Chicken Stock
- Coconut Milk
- Dijon Mustard
- Honey
- Light Ranch Dressing
- Maple Syrup
- Mayonnaise, low-fat
- Red Wine Vinegar
- Rice Vinegar
- Soy Sauce
- Sweet Pickle Relish
- Tarragon Vinegar
- Tomato Paste
- Tomato Sauce
- Tomato Puree
- Canned Tomato, diced, seedless

CHAPTER 4
CLEAR FLUIDS

BE PART OF THIS COMMUNITY OF CRAZY INNOVATORS AND
SHARE YOUR UNCONVENTIONAL KNOWLEDGE...BE PART OF ...
FUN CLUB KITCHEN

Breakfast

1. STRAWBERRY APPLE JUICE

Preparation Time: 5 minutes
Cooking Time: 0 minutes
Servings: 8-10 oz.

Ingredients:
- 2 cups strawberries (tops removed)
- 1 red apple, peeled, seeded, cored, and chopped
- 1 tablespoon chia seeds
- 1 cup water

Directions:
1. Set all the ingredients into your blender and pulse.
2. Set a fine-mesh strainer in a bowl. Before transferring your juice into the strainer.
3. Gently, press the pulp to extract all possible liquid, then discard it.
4. Add in your chia seeds, then leave to sit for at least 5 minutes.
5. Serve over ice. Enjoy!

Nutrition:
- Calories: 245
- Fat: 5 g
- Carbs: 52 g
- Fiber: 7 g
- Protein: 4 g

2. FALL ENERGIZER JUICE

Preparation Time: 10 minutes
Cooking Time: 0 minutes
Servings: 2

Ingredients:
- 2 pears, peeled, seeded, and chopped
- 2 Ambrosia apples, peeled, cored, and chopped
- 2 Granny Smith apples, peeled, cored, chopped
- 2 mandarins, juiced
- 2 cups sweet potato, peeled and chopped
- 1 pint cape gooseberries
- 2 inches ginger root, peeled

Directions:
1. Set all the ingredients into your blender and pulse.
2. Set a fine-mesh strainer in a bowl. Before transferring your juice into the strainer.
3. Gently, press the pulp to extract all possible liquid, then discard it.
4. Serve over ice. Enjoy!

Nutrition:
- Calories: 170
- Fat: 3 g
- Carbs: 33 g
- Fiber: 9 g
- Protein: 4 g

3. MUSHROOM, CAULIFLOWER AND CABBAGE BROTH

Preparation Time: 10 minutes
Cooking Time: 50 minutes
Servings: 2

Ingredients:
- 1 large yellow onion
- 1 cup celery stalks, chopped
- 2 carrots, diced or cubed
- 10 French beans
- ½ cabbage, diced
- 1-2 stalks celery leaves
- 1 ½ cup mushrooms, sliced
- 8 florets cauliflower
- 1 teaspoon garlic, chopped
- 1 teaspoon ginger, chopped
- 1 tablespoon oil
- 1 scallion stalk
- ½ teaspoon pepper, crushed

Directions:
1. Transfer all the ingredients to your stockpot. Top with enough water to cover, then allow to slowly come to a boil on high heat.
2. Switch to low heat and simmer for 50 minutes.
3. Set and pour the mixture through a fine-mesh strainer into a large bowl. Mash the vegetables well to extract all their juices.
4. Taste and season with salt. Enjoy.

Nutrition:
- Calories: 141
- Fat: 5 g
- Carbs: 22 g
- Fiber: 7 g
- Protein: 5 g

4. GINGER, MUSHROOM AND CAULIFLOWER BROTH

Preparation Time: 10 minutes
Cooking Time: 50 minutes
Servings: 3
Ingredients:
- 1 large yellow onion
- 1 cup celery stalks, chopped
- 2 carrots, diced or cubed
- 10 French beans
- 1 ginger root, peeled, diced, or grated
- 1-2 stalks celery leaves or coriander leaves
- 1 ½ cup mushrooms, sliced
- 8 florets cauliflower
- 1 teaspoon garlic, chopped
- 1 tablespoon oil
- 1 stalk spring onion greens or scallions
- ½ teaspoon crushed pepper or ground pepper

Directions:
1. Transfer all the ingredients to your stockpot. Top with enough water to cover, then allow to slowly come to a boil on high heat.
2. Switch to low heat and simmer for at least 50 minutes.
3. Set and pour the mixture through a fine-mesh strainer into a large bowl. Taste and season with salt.
4. Serve hot. Enjoy!

Nutrition:
- Calories: 141
- Fat: 5 g
- Carbs: 22 g
- Fiber: 7 g
- Protein: 5 g

5. FISH BROTH

Preparation Time: 15 minutes
Cooking Time: 45 minutes
Servings: 3
Ingredients:
- 1 large onion, chopped
- 1 large carrot chopped
- 1 fennel bulb and fronds, chopped (optional)
- 3 celery stalks, chopped
- Salt
- 2-5 pounds fish bones and heads
- 1 handful dried mushrooms (optional)

Directions:
1. Transfer the bones and vegetables to your stockpot. Top with enough water to cover, then allow to slowly come to a boil on high heat.
2. Set to low heat and simmer for 45 minutes.
3. Set and pour the mixture through a fine-mesh strainer into a large bowl. Taste and season with salt.
4. Serve hot. Enjoy!

Nutrition:
- Calories: 29
- Fat: 1 g
- Carbs: 2 g
- Fiber: 1 g
- Protein: 1 g

6. CLEAR PUMPKIN BROTH

Preparation Time: 15 minutes
Cooking Time: 30 minutes
Servings: 6
Ingredients:
- 6 cups water
- 2 tablespoons ginger, minced
- 2 cups potatoes, peeled and diced
- 3 cups kabocha, peeled and diced
- 1 carrot, peeled and diced
- 1 onion, diced
- ½ cup scallions, chopped
- 2 Pounds pork Bones

Directions:
1. Transfer the bones and vegetables to your stockpot. Top with enough water to cover, then allow to slowly come to a boil on high heat.

2. Switch to low heat and simmer for at least 30 minutes.
3. Set and pour the mixture through a fine-mesh strainer into a large bowl. Taste and season with salt.
4. Serve hot. Enjoy!

Nutrition:
- Calories: 216
- Fat: 1 g
- Carbs: 37 g
- Fiber: 4 g
- Protein: 8 g

7. PORK STOCK

Preparation Time: 15 minutes
Cooking Time: 12 hours
Servings: 8
Ingredients:
- 2 Pounds pork bones, roasted
- 1 onion, chopped in quarters
- 2 celery stalks, chopped in half
- 2 carrots, chopped in half
- 3 whole garlic cloves
- 1 tablespoon salt
- Filtered water (enough to cover bones)

Directions:
1. Transfer the bones and vegetables to your stockpot. Top with enough water to cover, then allow to slowly come to a boil on high heat.
2. Set to low heat and simmer for 12 hours.
3. Set and pour the mixture through a fine-mesh strainer into a large bowl. Taste and season with salt.
4. Serve hot. Enjoy!

Nutrition:
- Calories: 69
- Fat: 4 g
- Carbs: 1 g
- Fiber: 0.1 g
- Protein: 6 g

8. SLOW COOKER PORK BONE BROTH

Preparation Time: 15 minutes
Cooking Time: 24 hours
Servings: 12
Ingredients:
- 2 pounds pork bones, roasted
- ½ onion, chopped
- 2 medium carrots, chopped
- 1 stalk celery, chopped
- 2 whole garlic cloves
- 1 bay leaf
- 1 tablespoon sea salt
- 1 teaspoon peppercorns
- ¼ cup apple cider vinegar
- Filtered water (enough to cover bones)

Directions:
1. Transfer all the ingredients to your slow cooker. Top with enough water to cover, then allow to slowly come to a boil on high heat.
2. Switch to low heat and simmer for at least 24 hours.
3. Set and pour the mixture through a fine-mesh strainer into a large bowl. Taste and season with salt.
4. Serve hot. Enjoy!

Nutrition:
- Calories: 65
- Fat: 2 g
- Carbs: 7 g
- Fiber: 4 g
- Protein: 6 g

9. HOMEMADE NO PULP ORANGE JUICE

Preparation Time: 5 mins.
Cooking Time: 0 mins.
Servings: 1 ½ cups
Ingredients:
Oranges (4)

Directions:
Lightly squeeze the oranges on a hard surface to soften the exterior. Slice each in half.

Squeeze each orange over a fine mesh strainer.

Gently press the pulp to extract all possible liquid.

Serve over ice. Enjoy!

Nutrition:
50 calories, 0.2 g fat, 11.5 g carbs, g fiber, 0.8 g protein

10. APPLE ORANGE JUICE

Preparation Time: 5 mins.
Cooking Time: 0 mins.
Servings: 2
Ingredients:

Apple (1 Gala, peeled, cored, sliced)
Oranges (2, peeled, halved, seeded)
Honey (2 tsp, optional)
Water (3/4 cup)

Directions:

Squeeze each orange over a fine mesh strainer.

Gently press the pulp to extract as much liquid as possible.

Add in your apple, water, and orange juice in your blender and blend.

Set a fine mesh strainer a bowl. Before transferring your juice into the strainer.

Once again, gently press the pulp to remove all possible liquid then discard pulp.

Stir in your honey then serve over ice.

Nutrition:

180 calories, 1 g fat, 43 g carbs, 1 g fiber, 2 g protein

11. PINEAPPLE MINT JUICE

Preparation Time: 5 mins.
Cooking Time: 0 mins.
Servings: 4
Ingredients:

Pineapple (3 cups, cored and sliced, chunks)
Mint leaves (10 to 12, or to taste)
Sugar, or to taste (2 tablespoons, optional)
Water (1 1/2 cups)
Ice cubes (1 cup)

Directions:

Add all your ingredients into your blender, and blend.

Set a fine mesh strainer a bowl. Before transferring your juice into the strainer.

Gently press the pulp to extract all possible liquid then discard pulp.

Serve over ice. Enjoy!

Nutrition:

78 calories, 1 g fat, 22 g carbs, 2 g fiber, 1 g protein

Lunch

12. HOMEY CLEAR CHICKEN BROTH

Preparation Time: 10 minutes
Cooking Time: 3 ¼ hours
Servings: 6 cups
Ingredients:
- 2 lbs. chicken neck (2 lbs)
- 2 celery ribs with leaves (cut into chunks)
- 2 medium carrots (cut into chunks)
- 2 medium onions (quartered)
- 8-10 whole peppercorns
- 2 quarts cold water

Directions:
1. Transfer the bones and vegetables to your stockpot. Top with enough water to cover, then allow to slowly come to a boil on high heat.
2. Switch to low heat and simmer for at least 2 hours and up to 12 hours. (The longer it cooks, the more flavor you will get.)
3. Carefully pour the mixture through a fine-mesh strainer into a large bowl. Taste and season with salt.
4. Serve hot.

Nutrition:
- Calories: 245
- Fat: 14 g
- Carbs: 8 g
- Fiber: 2 g
- Protein: 21 g

13. ASIAN INSPIRED WONTON BROTH

Preparation Time: 5 minutes
Cooking Time: 1 hour 35 minutes
Servings: 1 gallon
Ingredients:
- 1 chicken thigh (skin on)
- 1 carrot (coarsely chopped)
- 1 stalk celery (coarsely chopped)
- 1 small onion (quartered)
- 3 dime-sized ginger (pieces)
- 2 tablespoons Kosher salt
- ¼ teaspoon turmeric
- 1/8 teaspoon MSG (don't leave it out)
- 5 white peppercorns (black can be substituted)
- 1 gallon water

Directions:
1. Transfer all your ingredients to your stockpot. Top with enough water to cover, then allow to slowly come to a boil on high heat.
2. Switch to low heat and simmer for at least 1 hour and 30 minutes.
3. Carefully pour the mixture through a fine-mesh strainer into a large bowl. Taste and season with salt.
4. Serve hot.

Nutrition:
- Calories: 181
- Fat: 7 g
- Carbs: 14 g
- Fiber: 1 g
- Protein: 14 g

14 OXTAIL BONE BROTH

Preparation Time: 15 minutes
Cooking Time: 12 hours
Servings: 8 cups
Ingredients:
- 2 lbs. oxtail
- 1 onion (chopped in quarters)
- 2 celery stalks (chopped in half)
- 2 carrots (chopped in half)
- 3 garlic cloves (whole)
- 1 tablespoon salt
- ½ tablespoon peppercorns
- Filtered water (enough to cover bones)

Directions:
1. Transfer the bones and vegetables to your stockpot. Top with enough water to cover, then allow to slowly come to a boil on high heat.
2. Switch to low heat and simmer for at least 2 hours and up to 12 hours. (The longer it cooks, the more flavor you will get.)
3. Carefully pour the mixture through a fine-mesh strainer into a large bowl. Taste and season with salt.

4. Serve hot.

Nutrition:
- Calories: 576
- Fat: 48 g
- Carbs: 8 g
- Fiber: 0 g
- Protein: 24 g

15. BEEF BONE BROTH

Preparation Time: 15 minutes
Cooking Time: 12 hours
Servings: 8 cups

Ingredients:
- 2 lbs. beef bones
- 1 onion (chopped in quarters)
- 2 celery stalks (chopped in half)
- 2 carrots (chopped in half)
- 3 garlic cloves (whole)
- 1 tablespoon salt
- ½ tablespoon peppercorns
- Filtered water (enough to cover bones)

Directions:
1. Transfer the bones and vegetables to your stockpot. Top with enough water to cover then allow to slowly come to a boil on high heat.
2. Switch to low heat and simmer for at least 2 hours and up to 12 hours. (The longer it cooks, the more flavor you will get.)
3. Carefully pour the mixture through a fine-mesh strainer into a large bowl. Taste and season with salt.
4. Serve hot.

Nutrition:
- Calories: 69
- Fat: 4 g
- Carbs: 1 g
- Fiber: 0.1 g
- Protein: 6 g

16. INDIAN INSPIRED VEGETABLE STOCK

Preparation Time: 15 minutes
Cooking Time: 11 minutes
Servings: 3 cups

Ingredients:
- ¾ cup onions (roughly chopped)
- ¾ cup carrot (roughly chopped)
- ¾ cup tomatoes (roughly chopped)
- ¾ cup potatoes (roughly chopped)
- 1 teaspoon turmeric
- Salt to taste

Directions:
1. Transfer your ingredients to your stockpot. Top with enough water to cover, then allow to slowly come to a boil on high heat.
2. Switch to low heat and simmer for 11 minutes.
3. Carefully pour the mixture through a fine-mesh strainer into a large bowl. Taste and season with salt.
4. Serve hot. Enjoy!

Nutrition:
- Calories: 103
- Fat: 0.2 mg
- Carbs: 23.3 g
- Fiber: 3.1 g
- Protein: 2.2 g

Snacks

17. THREE INGREDIENT SUGAR-FREE GELATIN

Preparation Time: 5 minutes
Cooking Time: 4 hours
Servings: 6-8
Ingredients:
- ¼ cup water (room temperature)
- ¼ cup water (hot)
- 1 tablespoon gelatin
- 1 cup orange juice (unsweetened)

Directions:
1. Combine your gelatin and room temperature water, stirring until fully dissolved.
2. Stir in your hot water, then leave to rest for about 2 minutes.
3. Add in your juice and stir until combined.
4. Transfer to serving size containers, then place on a tray in the refrigerator to set for about 4 hours.
5. Enjoy!

Nutrition:
- Calories: 17
- Fat: 0 g
- Carbs: 4 g
- Fiber: 0 g
- Protein: 0 g

18. CRANBERRY KOMBUCHA JELL-O

Preparation Time: 5 minutes
Cooking Time: 4 hours
Servings: 6
Ingredients:
- ¼ cup water (room temperature)
- ¼ cup hot water
- 1 tablespoon gelatin
- 1 cup cranberry kombucha (unsweetened)

Directions:
1. Combine your gelatin and room temperature water, stirring until fully dissolved.
2. Stir in your hot water, then leave to rest for about 2 minutes.
3. Add in your kombucha and stir until combined.
4. Transfer to serving size containers, then place on a tray in the refrigerator to set for about 4 hours.
5. Enjoy!

Nutrition:
- Calories: 13
- Fat: 0 g
- Carbs: 1 g
- Fiber: 0 g
- Protein: 0 g

19. STRAWBERRY GUMMIES

Preparation Time: 5 minutes
Cooking Time: 4 hours
Servings: 20-40 mini gummies
Ingredients:
- 1 cup strawberries (hulled, chopped)
- ¾ cup water
- 2 tablespoons gelatin

Directions:
1. Set your water and berries on to boil on high heat. Remove from heat as soon as the mixture begins to boil.
2. Transfer to your blender and blend. Add in your gelatin, then blend once more.
3. Pour your mixture into a silicone gummy mold.
4. Place on a tray in the refrigerator to set for about 4 hours.
5. Enjoy!

Nutrition:
- Calories: 3
- Fat: 0 g
- Carbs: 0 g
- Fiber: 0 g
- Protein: 0 g

20. FRUITY JELL-O STARS

Preparation Time: 15 minutes
Cooking Time: 5 minutes
Servings: 4

Ingredients:
- 1 tablespoon gelatin (powdered)
- ¾ cup boiling water
- 3 ½ fruit
- 1 tablespoon honey
- 1 teaspoon lemon juice

Directions:
1. Add all your ingredients into your blender and blend. Add in your gelatin, then blend once more.
2. Pour your mixture into a silicone gummy mold.
3. Place on a tray in the refrigerator to set for about 4 hours.
4. Enjoy!

Nutrition:
- Calories: 73
- Fat: 2 g
- Carbs: 14 g
- Fiber: 0 g
- Protein: 1 g

21. PLUM AND NECTARINE GELATIN PUDDING

Preparation Time: 15 minutes
Cooking Time: 0 minutes
Servings: 5

Ingredients:
- 1 nectarine (large)
- 2 plums (small)
- 2 tablespoons gelatin
- 1 ½ cup water (room temp.)
- 2 cups boiling water
- 2 teaspoons lemon juice
- 1/3 cup honey
- 1 tablespoon vanilla
- 1/8 teaspoon sea salt

Directions:
1. Add your fruits in your blend to puree until smooth with room temperature water, lemon juice, and vanilla until smooth.
2. Strain through a fine-mesh strainer.
3. Combine your gelatin and fruit mixture, stirring until fully dissolved.
4. Stir in your hot water, then leave to rest for about 2 minutes.
5. Add in your remaining ingredients and stir until combined.
6. Transfer to serving size containers, then place on a tray in the refrigerator to set for about 4 hours. Enjoy!

Nutrition:
- Calories: 157
- Fat: 5 g
- Carbs: 26 g
- Fiber: 1 g
- Protein: 3 g

22. HOMEMADE LEMON GELATIN

Preparation Time: 2 hours 5 minutes
Cooking Time: 0 minutes
Servings: 8

Ingredients:
- 3 tablespoons gelatin (granulated)
- 1½ cup stevia
- 1 1/2 cup boiling water
- 3 cups Room temperature Water
- 1 1/8 cup Lemon Juice
- ½ teaspoon Lemon zest

Directions:
1. Combine your gelatin and room temperature water, stirring until fully dissolved.
2. Stir in your hot water, then leave to rest for about 2 minutes.
3. Add in your remaining ingredients and stir until combined.
4. Transfer to serving size containers, then place on a tray in the refrigerator to set for about 4 hours. Enjoy!

Nutrition:
- Calories: 68
- Fat: 0 g
- Carbs: 1 g
- Fiber: 0 g
- Protein: 2 g

23. SOUR BLUEBERRY GUMMIES

Preparation Time: 5 minutes.
Cooking Time: 5 minutes.
Servings: 9

Ingredients:

- 1 ½ cup blueberries
- 1/3 cup gelatin (grass-fed)
- Water

Directions:
1. Set your water and berries on to boil on high heat. Remove from heat as soon as the mixture begins to boil.
2. Transfer to your blender and blend. Add in your gelatin, then blend once more.
3. Pour your mixture into a silicone gummy mold.
4. Place on a tray in the refrigerator to set for about 4 hours. Enjoy!

Nutrition:
- Calories: 73
- Fat: 2 g
- Carbs: 14 g
- Fiber: 0 g
- Protein: 1 g

24 SUGAR-FREE CINNAMON JELLY

Preparation Time: 2 hours 15 minutes
Cooking Time: 0 minutes
Servings: 2
Ingredients:
- 1 cup room temperature water
- 2 teaspoons gelatin
- 1/2 cup apple Juice

Directions:
1. Combine your gelatin and room temperature water, stirring until fully dissolved.
2. Stir in your hot water, then leave to rest for about 2 minutes.
3. Add in your apple juice and stir until combined.
4. Transfer to serving size containers, then place on a tray in the refrigerator to set for about 4 hours.
5. Enjoy!

Nutrition:
- Calories: 35
- Fat: 0 g
- Carbs: 17 g
- Fiber: 0 g
- Protein: 0 g

Dinner

25. CHICKEN VEGETABLE SOUP

Preparation Time: 23 minutes
Cooking Time: 15 minutes
Servings: 8
Ingredients:
- 2 tablespoons avocado oil
- 1 small yellow onion, peeled and chopped
- 2 large carrots, peeled and chopped
- 2 large stalks celery, ends removed and sliced
- 3 garlic cloves, minced
- 1 teaspoon dried thyme
- 1 teaspoon salt
- 8 cups chicken stock
- 3 boneless, skinless, frozen chicken breasts

Directions:
1. Heat the oil for 1 minute. Add the onion, carrots, and celery and saute for 8 minutes.
2. Add the garlic, thyme, and salt, then saute for another 30 seconds. Press the Cancel button.
3. Add the stock and frozen chicken breasts to the pot. Secure the lid.
4. Pressure cook and adjust the time to 6 minutes.
5. Allow cooling into bowls to serve.

Nutrition:
- Calories: 209
- Fat: 7 g
- Protein: 21 g
- Sodium: 687 mg
- Fiber: 1 g
- Carbs: 12 g
- Sugar: 5 g

26. CARROT GINGER SOUP

Preparation Time: 20 minutes
Cooking Time: 21 minutes
Servings: 4
Ingredients:
- 1 tablespoon avocado oil
- 1 large yellow onion, peeled and chopped

- 1 pound carrots, peeled and chopped
- 1 tablespoon fresh ginger, peeled and minced
- 1 ½ teaspoon salt
- 3 cups vegetable broth

Directions:
1. Add the oil to the inner pot, allowing it to heat for 1 minute.
2. Attach the onion, carrots, ginger, and salt, then saute for 5 minutes.
3. Press the Cancel button.
4. Add the broth and secure the lid. Adjust the time to 15 minutes.
5. Allow the soup to cool a few minutes, and then transfer it to a large blender.
6. Merge on high until smooth and then serve.

Nutrition:
- Calories: 99
- Fat: 4 g
- Protein: 1 g
- Sodium: 1,348 mg
- Fiber: 4 g
- Carbs: 16 g
- Sugar: 7 g

27. TURKEY SWEET POTATO HASH

Preparation Time: 10 minutes
Cooking Time: 12 minutes
Servings: 4
Ingredients:
- 1 ½ tablespoon avocado oil
- 1 medium yellow onion, peeled and diced
- 2 garlic cloves, minced
- 1 medium sweet potato, cut into cubes (peeling not necessary)
- ½ pound lean ground turkey
- ½ teaspoon salt
- 1 teaspoon Italian seasoning blend

Directions:
1. Pour the oil and allow it to heat for 1 minute.
2. Add the onion and cook until softened, about 5 minutes. Add the garlic and cook for an additional 30 seconds.
3. Add the sweet potato, turkey, salt, and Italian seasoning and cook for another 5 minutes.

Nutrition:
- Calories: 172
- Fat: 9 g
- Protein: 12 g
- Sodium: 348 mg
- Fiber: 1 g
- Carbs: 10 g
- Sugar: 3 g

28. CHICKEN TENDERS WITH HONEY MUSTARD SAUCE

Preparation Time: 5 minutes
Cooking Time: 10 minutes
Servings: 4
Ingredients:
- 1 lb. chicken tenders
- 1 tablespoon fresh thyme leaves
- 1/2 teaspoon salt
- 1/4 teaspoon black pepper
- 1 tablespoon avocado oil
- 1 cup chicken stock
- 1/4 cup Dijon mustard
- 1/4 cup raw honey

Directions:
1. Dry the chicken tenders with a towel and then season them with thyme, salt, and pepper.
2. Attach the oil and let it heat for 2 minutes.
3. Add the chicken tenders and seer them until brown on both sides, about 1 minute per side. Press the Cancel button.
4. Remove the chicken tenders and set them aside.
5. Add the stock to the pot. Use a spoon to scrape up any small bits from the bottom of the pot.
6. Set the steam rack in the inner pot and place the chicken tenders directly on the rack.
7. While the chicken is cooking, prepare the sauce.
8. In a bowl, combine the Dijon mustard and honey, then stir to combine.
9. Serve the chicken tenders with the honey mustard sauce.

Nutrition:
- Calories: 223
- Fat: 5 g

- Protein: 22 g
- Sodium: 778 mg
- Fiber: 0 g
- Carbs: 19 g
- Sugar: 18 g

29. CHICKEN BREASTS WITH CABBAGE AND MUSHROOMS

Preparation Time: 10 minutes
Cooking Time: 18 minutes
Servings: 4
Ingredients:
- 2 tablespoons avocado oil
- 1 pound sliced Baby Bella mushrooms
- 1 ½ teaspoon salt, divided
- 2 garlic cloves, minced
- 8 cups chopped green cabbage
- 1 ½ teaspoon dried thyme
- ½ cup chicken stock
- 1 ½ pound boneless, skinless chicken breasts

Directions:
1. Add the oil. Allow it to heat for 1 minute. Attach the mushrooms and 1/4 teaspoon of salt. Saute until they have cooked down and released their liquid, about 10 minutes.
2. Add the garlic and saute for another 30 seconds. Press the Cancel button.
3. Attach the cabbage, ¼ teaspoon of salt, thyme, and the stock to the inner pot. Stir to combine.
4. Dry the chicken breasts and sprinkle both sides with the remaining salt. Place on top of the cabbage mixture.
5. Transfer to plates and spoon the juices on top.

Nutrition:
- Calories: 337
- Fat: 10 g
- Protein: 44 g
- Sodium: 1,023 mg
- Fiber: 4 g
- Carbs: 14 g
- Sugar: 2 g

30. DUCK WITH BOK CHOY

Preparation Time: 15 minutes
Cooking Time: 12 minutes
Servings: 6
Ingredients:
- 2 tablespoons coconut oil
- 1 onion, sliced thinly
- 2 teaspoons fresh ginger, grated finely
- 2 minced garlic cloves
- 1 tablespoon fresh orange zest, grated finely
- ¼ cup chicken broth
- 2/3 cup fresh orange juice
- 1 roasted duck, meat picked
- 3 pounds bok choy leaves
- 1 orange, peeled, seeded, and segmented

Directions:
1. In a sizable skillet, melt the coconut oil on medium heat. Attach the onion, saute for around 3 minutes. Add ginger and garlic, then saute for about 1-2 minutes.
2. Stir in the orange zest, broth, and orange juice.
3. Add the duck meat and cook for around 3 minutes.
4. Transfer the meat pieces to a plate. Add the bok choy and cook for about 3-4 minutes.
5. Divide the bok choy mixture into serving plates and top with duck meat.
6. Serve with the garnishing of orange segments.

Nutrition:
- Calories: 290
- Fat: 4 g
- Fiber: 6 g
- Carbs: 8 g
- Protein: 14 g

31. BEEF WITH MUSHROOM AND BROCCOLI

Preparation Time: 60 minutes
Cooking Time: 2 minutes
Servings: 4
Ingredients:
For Beef Marinade:
- 1 garlic clove, minced
- 1 piece fresh ginger, minced
- Salt and freshly ground black pepper
- 3 tablespoons white wine vinegar
- ¾ cup beef broth
- 1 pound flank steak, trimmed and sliced into thin strips

For Vegetables:
- 2 tablespoons coconut oil
- 2 garlic cloves
- 3 cups broccoli rabe
- 4 oz. shiitake mushrooms
- 8 oz. cremini mushrooms

Directions:

For the marinade:
1. In a substantial bowl, mix all ingredients except the beef. Add it and coat with the marinade generously. Refrigerate to soak for around ¼ hour.
2. In a substantial skillet, warm oil on medium-high heat.
3. Detach the beef from the bowl, reserving the marinade.

For the Vegetables:
1. Attach the beef and garlic and cook for about 3-4 minutes or till browned.
2. In the same skillet, add the reserved marinade, broccoli, and mushrooms. Cook for approximately 3-4 minutes.
3. Set in the beef and cook for about 3-4 minutes.

Nutrition:
- Calories: 200
- Carbs: 31 g
- Cholesterol: 93 mg
- Fat: 4 g
- Protein: 10 g
- Fiber: 2 g

32. BEEF WITH ZUCCHINI NOODLES

Preparation Time: 15 minutes
Cooking Time: 9 minutes
Servings: 4

Ingredients:
- 1 teaspoon fresh ginger, grated
- 2 medium garlic cloves, minced
- 1/4 cup coconut aminos
- 2 tablespoons fresh lime juice
- 1½ pound NY strip steak, trimmed and sliced thinly
- 2 medium zucchini, spiralized with blade C
- Salt to taste
- 3 tablespoons essential olive oil
- 2 medium scallions, sliced
- 1 teaspoon red pepper flakes, crushed
- 2 tablespoons fresh cilantro, chopped

Directions:
1. In a big bowl, merge ginger, garlic, coconut aminos, and lime juice. Add the beef and coat with the marinade generously. Refrigerate to soak for approximately 10 minutes.
2. Set zucchini noodles over a large paper towel and sprinkle with salt.
3. Keep aside for around 10 minutes.
4. In a big skillet, heat oil on medium-high heat. Attach the scallions, and red pepper flakes, then saute for about 1 minute.
5. Attach the beef with the marinade and stir-fry for around 3-4 minutes or until browned.
6. Stir in the fresh cilantro, then add the zucchini and cook for approximately 3-4 minutes. Serve hot.

Nutrition:
- Calories: 1366
- Carbs: 166 g
- Cholesterol: 6 mg
- Fat: 67 g
- Protein: 59 g
- Fiber: 41 g

33. SPICED GROUND BEEF
by Deborah A. Andrade – Aberdeen

Preparation Time: 10 minutes
Cooking Time: 22 minutes
Servings: 5

Ingredients:
- 2 tablespoons coconut oil
- 2 whole cloves
- 2 whole cardamoms
- 1 (2 inches) piece cinnamon stick
- 2 bay leaves
- 1 teaspoon cumin seeds
- 2 onions, chopped
- Salt to taste
- ½ tablespoon garlic paste
- ½ tablespoon fresh ginger paste
- 1 pound lean ground beef
- 1½ teaspoon fennel seeds powder

- 1 teaspoon ground cumin
- 1 ½ teaspoon red chili powder
- 1/8 teaspoon ground turmeric
- Freshly ground black pepper, to taste
- 1 cup coconut milk
- ¼ cup water
- ¼ cup fresh cilantro, chopped

Directions:

1. In a sizable pan, warm oil on medium heat. Mix cloves, cardamoms, cinnamon sticks, bay leaves, and cumin seeds; cook for about 20 seconds.
2. Attach the onion, and 2 pinches of salt, then saute for about 3-4 minutes.
3. Add the garlic-ginger paste and stir-fry for about 2 minutes.
4. Attach the beef and cook for about 4-5 minutes, entering pieces using the spoon. Stir in spices and cook.
5. Set in the coconut milk and water; cook for about 7-8 minutes. Flavor with salt and take away from the heat.
6. Serve hot using the garnishing of cilantro.

Nutrition:
- Calories: 216
- Protein: 8.83 g
- Fat: 11.48 g
- Carbs: 21.86 g

34. GROUND BEEF WITH VEGGIES
by Shirley Scott – Clearwater

Preparation Time: 60 minutes
Cooking Time: 22 minutes
Servings: 4

Ingredients:
- 1-2 tablespoons coconut oil
- 1 red onion
- 2 red jalapeño peppers
- 2 minced garlic cloves
- 1 pound lean ground beef
- 1 small head broccoli, chopped
- ½ head cauliflower
- 3 carrots, peeled and sliced
- 3 celery ribs
- Chopped fresh thyme to taste
- Dried sage to taste
- Ground turmeric to taste
- Salt and freshly ground black pepper

Directions:

1. In a large skillet, dissolve the coconut oil on medium heat.
2. Stir in the onion, jalapeño peppers, and garlic. Saute for about 5 minutes.
3. Attach the beef and cook for around 4-5 minutes, entering pieces using the spoon.
4. Add the remaining ingredients and cook, stirring occasionally for about 8-10 minutes. Serve hot.

Nutrition:
- Calories: 141
- Cholesterol: 50 mg
- Carbs: 6 g
- Fat: 1 g
- Sugar: 3 g
- Fiber: 2 g

Dinner

35. GALA APPLE FLAVORED ICE CUBES

Preparation Time: 4 hours 10 minutes
Cooking Time: 0 minutes
Servings: 24 ice cubes

Ingredients:
- 2 Gala apple
- 4 teaspoons honey
- 3 cups water

Directions:
1. Add all your ingredients into your blender, and blend.
2. Set a fine-mesh strainer in a bowl. Before transferring your juice into the strainer.
3. Gently press the pulp to extract all possible liquid, then discard the pulp.
4. Fill your empty ice trays with your juice.
5. Set to freeze for at least 3 hours until frozen.
6. Transfer your flavored ice cubes to freezer bags.
7. Keep them in the freezer until ready to serve.

Nutrition:
- Calories: 83
- Fat: 1 g
- Carbs: 21 g
- Fiber: 2 g
- Protein: 1 g

36. KALE FLAVORED ICE CUBES

Preparation Time: 4 hours 10 minutes
Cooking Time: 0 minutes
Servings: 24 ice cubes

Ingredients:
- ¼ cup honey
- 2 cups water
- 3 cups kale (chopped)

Directions:
1. Add all your ingredients into your blender, and blend.
2. Set a fine-mesh strainer in a bowl. Before transferring your juice into the strainer.
3. Gently press the pulp to extract all possible liquid, then discard the pulp.
4. Fill your empty ice trays with your juice.
5. Set to freeze for at least 3 hours until frozen.
6. Transfer your flavored ice cubes to freezer bags.
7. Keep them in the freezer until ready to serve.

Nutrition:
- Calories: 110
- Fat: 1 g
- Carbs: 25 g
- Fiber: 4 g
- Protein: 3 g

37. CRANBERRY FLAVORED ICE CUBES

Preparation Time: 4 hours 10 minutes
Cooking Time: 0 minutes
Servings: 24 ice cubes

Ingredients:
- 3 cups cranberry juice unsweetened)

Directions:
1. Fill your empty ice trays with your juice.
2. Set to freeze for at least 3 hours until frozen.
3. Transfer your flavored ice cubes to freezer bags.
4. Keep them in the freezer until ready to serve.

Nutrition:
- Calories: 120
- Fat: 2 g
- Carbs: 24 g
- Fiber: 1 g
- Protein: 0 g

38. BANANA ICE CUBES

Preparation Time: 15 minutes
Cooking Time: 0 minutes
Servings: 24 ice cubes

Ingredients:
- 2 bananas (peeled, sliced)
- 1 tablespoon honey

- 3 cups water

Directions:
1. Add all your ingredients into your blender, and blend.
2. Set a fine-mesh strainer in a bowl. Before transferring your juice into the strainer.
3. Gently press the pulp to extract all possible liquid, then discard the pulp.
4. Fill your empty ice trays with your juice.
5. Set to freeze for at least 3 hours until frozen.
6. Transfer your flavored ice cubes to freezer bags.
7. Keep them in the freezer until ready to serve.

Nutrition:
- Calories: 71
- Fat: 0 g
- Carbs: 16 g
- Fiber: 1 g
- Protein: 2 g

39. ELDERBERRY GUMMIES

Preparation Time: 7 minutes
Cooking Time: 4 hours
Servings: 20-50
Ingredients:
- 2 tablespoons gelatin
- ¼ cup water (room temperature)
- ¼ cup hot water
- ½ cup orange juice
- 2 tablespoons lemon juice
- 2 tablespoons elderberry soothing syrup

Directions:
1. Combine your gelatin and room temperature water, stirring until fully dissolved.
2. Stir in your hot water, then leave to rest for about 2 minutes.
3. Add in your remaining ingredients and stir until combined.
4. Transfer to serving size containers, then place on a tray in the refrigerator to set for about 4 hours. Enjoy!

Nutrition:
- Calories: 3
- Fat: 0 g
- Carbs: 1 g
- Fiber: 0 g
- Protein: 0 g

40. BLACKBERRY-ROSE ICE POPS

Preparation Time: 25 minutes
Cooking Time: 5 hours
Servings: 10
Ingredients:
- 9 tablespoons cane sugar (organic)
- 9 tablespoons water (for simple syrup)
- 6 ½ cups blackberries
- 1 tablespoon lemon juice
- 1 teaspoon rosewater
- 1 cup water

Directions:
1. Create a simple syrup by heating sugar and the water for the simple syrup over medium heat.
2. Allow the mixture to simmer, stirring until the sugar dissolves. Set to cool (about 10 minutes).
3. Add all your ingredients into your blender, and blend.
4. Set a fine-mesh strainer in a bowl. Before transferring your juice into the strainer.
5. Gently press the pulp to extract all possible liquid, then discard the pulp.
6. Pour your juice into your ice-pop molds, filling each three-quarter of the way.
7. Add in your ice pop sticks, then set to freeze for at least 5 hours or until solid. Unmold and enjoy.

Nutrition:
- Calories: 112
- Fat: 0 g
- Carbs: 30 g
- Fiber: 5 g
- Protein: 1 g

41. FROZEN STRAWBERRY-PEACH POPS

Preparation Time: 5 minutes
Cooking Time: 0 minutes
Servings: 5
Ingredients:
- ½ cup sugar
- 6 oz. strawberries

- 6 oz. peaches
- 4 oz. water
- 1 tablespoon lemon juice

Directions:
1. Create a simple syrup by heating sugar and water over medium heat.
2. Allow the mixture to simmer, stirring until the sugar dissolves. Set to cool (about 10 minutes).
3. Add all your ingredients into your blender, and blend.
4. Set a fine-mesh strainer in a bowl. Before transferring your juice into the strainer.
5. Gently press the pulp to extract all possible liquid, then discard the pulp.
6. Pour your juice into your ice-pop molds, filling each three-quarter of the way.
7. Add in your ice pop sticks, then set to freeze for at least 5 hours or until solid. Unmold and enjoy.

Nutrition:
- Calories: 102
- Fat: 1 g
- Carbs: 12 g
- Fiber: 2 g
- Protein: 2 g

42. HONEY LEMONADE POPSICLES
by Sandra Lamb - New Orleans

Preparation Time: 5 minutes
Cooking Time: 0 minutes
Servings: 8

Ingredients:
- ½ cup honey
- 12 oz. lemon juice
- 6 oz. water

Directions:
1. Create honey water by heating honey and over medium heat.
2. Allow the mixture to simmer, stirring until the honey melts. Set to cool (about 10 minutes).
3. In a spouted container, combine all your ingredients.
4. Pour your juice into your ice-pop molds, filling each three-quarter of the way.
5. Add in your ice pop sticks, then set to freeze for at least 5 hours or until solid. Unmold and enjoy.

Nutrition:
- Calories: 36
- Fat: 3 g
- Carbs: 3 g
- Fiber: 1 g
- Protein: 3 g

43. ORANGE STRAWBERRY POPSICLES
by Allison Howell - Eau Claire

Preparation Time: 10 minutes
Cooking Time: 0 minutes
Servings: 12 popsicles

Ingredients:
- 4 cups strawberry (hulled)
- 2 cups orange juice
- 1 lime (juiced)
- ¼ cup honey

Directions:
1. Add all your ingredients into your blender, and blend.
2. Set a fine-mesh strainer in a bowl. Before transferring your juice into the strainer.
3. Gently press the pulp to extract all possible liquid, then discard the pulp.
4. Pour your juice into your ice-pop molds, filling each three-quarter of the way.

Nutrition:
- Calories: 160
- Fat: 0 g
- Carbs: 40 g
- Fiber: 1 g
- Protein: 0 g

44. MELON BASIL MOSCOW MULE POPSICLES
by William Carpenter - West Mifflin

Preparation Time: 5 minutes
Cooking Time: 0 minutes
Servings: 10 popsicles

Ingredients:
- 1 lb. cantaloupe (peeled, seeded chopped)
- 7 leaves mint
- 4 oz. water

- 4 oz. limeade
- 16 oz. ginger beer
- 2 oz. simple syrup

Directions:

1. Add all your ingredients into your blender, and blend.
2. Set a fine-mesh strainer in a bowl. Before transferring your juice into the strainer.
3. Gently press the pulp to extract all possible liquid, then discard the pulp.
4. Pour your juice into your ice-pop molds, filling each three-quarter of the way.

Nutrition:
- Calories: 34
- Fat: 0 g
- Carbs: 8 g
- Fiber: 1 g
- Protein: 2 g

45. HONEYDEW MINT HOMEMADE POPSICLES

by Christine Pattison – Brattleboro

Preparation Time: 10 minutes
Cooking Time: 0 minutes
Servings: 10 popsicles

Ingredients:
- ½ honeydew melon (peeled, cubed)
- 1/3 cup granulated sugar
- 10 leaves mint
- 1 tablespoon lime juice
- 6 oz. water
- 1 pinch xanthan gum

Directions:

1. Add all your ingredients into your blender, and blend.
2. Set a fine-mesh strainer in a bowl. Before transferring your juice into the strainer.
3. Gently press the pulp to extract all possible liquid, then discard the pulp.
4. Pour your juice into your ice-pop molds, filling each three-quarter.

Nutrition:
- Calories: 34
- Fat: 0 g
- Carbs: 8 g
- Fiber: 1 g
- Protein: 2 g

CHAPTER 5
LOW RESIDUALS

BE PART OF THIS COMMUNITY OF CRAZY INNOVATORS AND SHARE YOUR UNCONVENTIONAL KNOWLEDGE...BE PART OF ...
FUN CLUB KITCHEN

Breakfast

46. BREAKFAST CEREAL

Preparation Time: 5 minutes
Cooking Time: 5 minutes
Servings: 4
Ingredients:
- 3 cups cooked old fashioned oatmeal
- 3 cups cooked quinoa
- 4 cups bananas, peeled and chopped

Directions:
1. Combine the oatmeal and quinoa; mix well.
2. Evenly, divide into 4 bowls and top with the bananas before serving.

Nutrition:
- Calories: 228
- Fat: 3 g
- Carbs: 43 g
- Fiber: 6 g
- Protein: 12 g

47. SWEET POTATO HASH WITH SAUSAGE AND SPINACH

Preparation Time: 5 minutes
Cooking Time: 15 minutes
Servings: 4
Ingredients:
- 4 small chopped sweet potatoes
- 2 apples, cored and chopped
- 1 garlic clove, minced
- 1 pound ground sausage
- 10 oz. chopped spinach
- Salt and pepper

Directions:
1. Brown the sausage until no pink remains. Add the remaining ingredients.
2. Cook until the spinach and apples are tender. Season to taste and serve hot.

Nutrition:
- Calories: 544
- Fat: 2 g
- Carbs: 65 g
- Fiber: 2 g
- Protein: 11 g

48. CAJUN OMELET

Preparation Time: 5 minutes
Cooking Time: 8 minutes
Servings: 2
Ingredients:
- ¼ lb. spicy sausage
- 1/3 cup sliced mushrooms
- ½ diced onion
- 4 large eggs
- ½ medium bell pepper, chopped
- 2 tablespoons water
- A pinch of cayenne pepper (optional)
- Sea salt and fresh pepper to taste
- 1 tablespoon mustard

Directions:
1. Brown the sausage in a saucepan until cooked through. Add the mushrooms, onion, and bell pepper. Cook for another 3-5 minutes, or until tender.
2. Meanwhile, whisk together the eggs, water, mustard, and spices. Season with salt and pepper.
3. Top with your eggs over, then reduce to low heat. Cook until the top is nearly set, and then fold the omelet in half and cover.
4. Cook for another minute before serving hot.

Nutrition:
- Calories: 467
- Fat: 14 g
- Carbs: 11 g
- Fiber: 2 g

48. STRAWBERRY CASHEW CHIA PUDDING

Preparation Time: 10 minutes
Cooking Time: 0 minutes
Servings: 2
Ingredients:
- 6 tablespoons chia seeds

- 2 cups cashew milk, unsweetened
- Strawberries for topping

Directions:
1. Merge the chia seeds and milk; mix well. Refrigerate overnight.
2. Stir in the berries and serve.

Nutrition:
- Calories: 223
- Fat: 12 g
- Carbs: 18 g
- Fiber: 2 g
- Protein: 10 g

50. PEANUT BUTTER BANANA OATMEAL

Preparation Time: 5 minutes
Cooking Time: 0 minutes
Servings: 1

Ingredients:
- 1/3 cup quick oats
- ¼ teaspoon cinnamon (optional)
- ½ sliced banana
- 1 tablespoon peanut butter, unsweetened

Directions:
1. Merge all ingredients in a bowl with a lid. Refrigerate.

Nutrition:
- Calories: 645
- Fat: 32 g
- Carbs: 65 g
- Fiber: 5 g
- Protein: 26 g

51. OVERNIGHT PEACH OATMEAL

Preparation Time: 10 minutes
Cooking Time: 0 minutes
Servings: 2

Ingredients:
- ½ cup old fashioned oats
- 2/3 cup skim milk
- ½ cup plain Greek yogurt
- 1 tablespoon chia seeds
- ½ teaspoon Vanilla
- ½ cup peach, peeled and diced
- 1 medium banana, peeled and chopped

Directions:
2. Combine the oats, milk, yogurt, chia seeds, and vanilla in a bowl with a lid.
3. Refrigerate for 12 hours.
4. Top with the fruits before serving.

Nutrition:
- Calories: 282
- Fat: 6 g
- Carbs: 48 g
- Fiber: 2 g
- Protein: 10 g

52. MEDITERRANEAN SALMON AND POTATO SALAD

Preparation Time: 15 minutes
Cooking Time: 18 minutes
Servings: 4

Ingredients:
- 1 lb. red potatoes, peeled and cut into wedges
- ½ cup + 2 tablespoons more extra-virgin olive oil
- 2 tablespoons balsamic vinegar
- 1 tablespoon fresh rosemary, minced
- 2 cups peas, cooked and drained
- 4 (4 oz. each) salmon fillets
- 2 tablespoons lemon juice
- ¼ teaspoon salt
- 2 cups English cucumber, sliced and seedless

Directions:
1. In a saucepan, set water to a boil and cook potatoes until tender, about 10 minutes.
2. Drain and set potatoes back into the pan. To make the dressing, in a bowl, set together 1/2 cup of olive oil, vinegar, and rosemary.
3. Combine potatoes and peas with the dressing. Set aside. In a separate medium pan, warm the remaining 2 tablespoons of olive oil over medium heat.
4. Attach salmon fillets and set with lemon juice and salt.
5. Cook on both sides or until fish flakes easily. To serve, place cucumber slices on a serving plate top with potato salad and fish fillets.

Nutrition:

- Calories: 463
- Fat: 4 g
- Carbs: 75 g
- Fiber: 18 g
- Protein: 34 g

53. PEA TUNA SALAD
by Randy Hipp – Manhattan

Preparation Time: 15 minutes
Cooking Time: 0 minutes
Servings: 4

Ingredients:
- 3 lbs. cooked peas
- ½ cup low-fat mayonnaise
- 1/3 cup tarragon vinegar
- 1 teaspoon honey Dijon mustard
- 2 small shallots, thinly sliced
- 2 (6 oz.) cans tuna fish, drained
- 2 small sprigs fresh tarragon, finely chopped

Directions:
1. In a large bowl, merge mayonnaise, vinegar, and mustard. Add tuna fish, shallots, and peas; toss to coat with dressing.
2. Secure and refrigerate for 1 hour before serving. Set with fresh tarragon and serve.

Nutrition:
- Calories: 246
- Fat: 13 g
- Carbs: 11 g
- Fiber: 1 g
- Protein: 22 g

54. CARROT AND TURKEY SOUP
by Charmaine J. Nowlin – West Allis

Preparation Time: 15 minutes
Cooking Time: 40 minutes
Servings: 4

Ingredients:
- ½ lb. lean ground turkey
- ½ bag frozen carrot
- ¼ cup green peas
- 1 can (32 oz.) chicken broth
- 2 medium tomatoes, seeded and roughly chopped
- 1 teaspoon garlic powder
- 1 teaspoon paprika
- 1 teaspoon oregano
- 1 bay leaf

Directions:
1. Over medium heat, set the ground turkey in a soup pot. Add peas, frozen carrot, paprika, tomatoes, garlic powder, bay leaf, oregano, and broth.
2. Set the pot to a boil, lower heat, cover, and simmer for 30 minutes.

Nutrition:
- Calories: 436
- Fat: 12 g
- Carbs: 20 g
- Fiber: 6 g
- Protein: 59 g

55. CREAMY PUMPKIN SOUP
by Wendy Carey – Cleghorn

Preparation Time: 15 minutes
Cooking Time: 1 hour 10 minutes
Servings: 4

Ingredients:
- 1 pumpkin, cut lengthwise, seeds removed and peeled
- 1 sweet potato, cut lengthwise and peeled
- 2 tablespoons olive oil
- 4 garlic cloves, unpeeled
- 4 cups vegetable stock
- ¼ cup light cream
- Salt
- 1 tablespoon chopped Shallots

Directions:
1. Preheat the oven to 375°F. Cut all the sides of the pumpkin, shallots, and sweet potato with oil.
2. Transfer your vegetables with the garlic to a roasting pan. Set to roast for about 40 minutes or until tender.
3. Let the vegetables cool for a time and scoop out the flesh of the sweet potato and pumpkin.
4. In a soup pot, place the flesh of roasted vegetables, shallots, and peeled garlic. Add the broth and set to a boil.
5. Set the heat, and let it simmer, covered for 30 minutes, stirring occasionally. Let the soup cool.

6. Set the soup with a hand blender until smooth. Add the cream.

7. Season to taste and simmer until warmed through, about 5 minutes. Serve in warm soup bowls.

Nutrition:
- Calories: 332
- Fat: 18 g
- Carbs: 32 g
- Fiber: 9 g
- Protein: 12 g

56 CHICKEN PEA SOUP
by Sandra Nelson – Tampa

Preparation Time: 15 minutes
Cooking Time: 55 minutes
Servings: 4

Ingredients:
- 1 lb. chicken breast, skinless, boneless, and cubed
- 2 tablespoons olive oil
- 3 garlic cloves, minced
- 3 carrots, grated
- 1 bay leaf
- 1 teaspoon salt
- 1 teaspoon poultry seasoning
- 8 cups chicken broth
- ½ cup dried split peas, washed and drained
- 1 cup green peas

Directions:

1. Warm up the olive oil over medium heat in a soup pot. Add the chicken and cook for 5 minutes until lightly browned.

2. Attach the garlic, bay leaf, carrots, salt, and seasoning. Cook until vegetables soften, stirring occasionally.

3. Pour the broth and split peas into the pot; bring to a boil. Set the heat, cover, and simmer on low heat for 30-45 minutes.

4. Stir in green peas to the soup and heat for 5 minutes, stirring to combine all ingredients.

Nutrition:
- Calories: 176
- Fat: 5 g
- Carbs: 18 g
- Fiber: 6 g
- Protein: 15 g

Lunch

57. GARDEN VEGGIES QUICHE

Preparation Time: 15 minutes
Cooking Time: 20 minutes
Servings: 4

Ingredients:
- 6 eggs
- ½ cup low-fat milk
- Salt and freshly ground black pepper, to taste
- 2 cup fresh baby spinach, chopped
- ½ cup green bell pepper, seeded and chopped
- 1 scallion, chopped
- ¼ cup fresh parsley, chopped
- 1 tablespoon fresh chives, minced

Directions:

1. Preheat the oven to 400°F. Lightly grease a pie dish.

2. In a bowl, add eggs, almond milk, salt, and black pepper and beat until well combined. Set aside.

3. In another bowl, add the vegetables and herbs and mix well.

4. In the bottom of the prepared pie dish, place the veggie mixture evenly and top with the egg mixture.

5. Bake for about 20 minutes or until a wooden skewer inserted in the center comes out clean.

6. Remove the pie dish from the oven and set it aside for about 5 minutes before slicing.

7. Cut into desired-sized wedges and serve warm.

Nutrition:
- Calories: 118
- Carbs: 4.3 g
- Protein: 10.1 g
- Fat: 7 g
- Sugar: 3 g
- Sodium: 160 mg
- Fiber: 0.8 g

58. FLUFFY PUMPKIN PANCAKES

Preparation Time: 10 minutes

Cooking Time: 40 minutes
Servings: 10
Ingredients:
- 2 eggs
- 1 cup buckwheat flour
- 1 tablespoon baking powder
- 1 teaspoon pumpkin pie spice
- ½ teaspoon salt
- 1 cup pumpkin puree
- ¾ cup + 2 tablespoons low-fat milk
- 3 tablespoons pure maple syrup
- 2 tablespoons olive oil
- 1 teaspoon vanilla extract

Directions:
1. In a blender, add all ingredients, and pulse until well combined.
2. Transfer the mixture into a bowl and set aside for about 10 minutes.
3. Heat a greased non-stick skillet over medium heat.
4. Place about ¼ cup of the mixture and spread in an even circle.
5. Cook for about 2 minutes per side.
6. Repeat with the remaining mixture.
7. Serve warm.

Nutrition:
- Calories: 113
- Carbs: 16.5 g
- Protein: 3.6 g
- Fat: 4.4 g
- Sugar: 5.9 g
- Sodium: 143 mg
- Fiber: 2 g

59. SUPER-TASTY CHICKEN MUFFINS

Preparation Time: 15 minutes
Cooking Time: 45 minutes
Servings: 8
Ingredients:
- 8 eggs
- Salt and freshly ground black pepper, as required
- 2 tablespoons filtered water
- 7 oz. cooked chicken, chopped finely
- 1½ cup fresh spinach, chopped
- 1 cup green bell pepper, seeded and chopped finely
- 2 tablespoons fresh parsley, chopped finely

Directions:
1. Preheat the oven to 350°F. Grease 8 cups of a muffin tin.
2. In a bowl, add eggs, salt, black pepper, and water and beat until well combined.
3. Add the chicken, spinach, bell pepper, and parsley and stir to combine.
4. Transfer the mixture into the prepared muffin cup evenly.
5. Bake for about 18-20 minutes or until golden brown.
6. Remove the muffin tin from the oven and place it onto a wire rack to cool for about 10 minutes.
7. Carefully invert the muffins onto a platter and serve warm.

Nutrition:
- Calories: 107
- Carbs: 1.7 g
- Protein: 13.1 g
- Fat: 5.2 g
- Sugar: 1.1 g
- Sodium: 102 mg
- Fiber: 0.4 g

60. CLASSIC ZUCCHINI BREAD

Preparation Time: 45 minutes
Cooking Time: 15 minutes
Servings: 24
Ingredients:
- 3 cups all-purpose flour
- 2 teaspoons baking soda
- 1 teaspoon ground cinnamon
- 1 teaspoon ground nutmeg
- 2 cups Splenda
- 1 cup olive oil
- 3 eggs, beaten
- 2 teaspoons vanilla extract
- 2 cups zucchini, peeled, seeded, and grated

Directions:

1. Preheat the oven to 325°F. Arrange a rack in the center of the oven. Grease 2 loaf pans.
2. In a medium bowl, mix the flour, baking soda, and spices.
3. In another large bowl, add the Splenda and oil and beat until well combined.
4. Add the eggs and vanilla extract and beat until well combined.
5. Add the flour mixture and mix until just combined.
6. Gently, fold in the zucchini.
7. Place the mixture into the bread loaf pans evenly.
8. Bake for about 45-50 minutes or until a toothpick inserted in the center of the bread comes out clean.
9. Remove the bread pans from the oven and place them onto a wire rack to cool for about 15 minutes.
10. Carefully, invert the pieces of bread onto the wire rack to cool completely before slicing.
11. With a sharp knife, cut each bread loaf into desired-sized slices and serve.

Nutrition:
- Calories: 219
- Carbs: 28.4 g
- Protein: 16.3 g
- Fat: 9.2 g
- Sugar: 16.3 g
- Sodium: 113 mg
- Fiber: 0.6 g

61. GREEK INSPIRED CUCUMBER SALAD

Preparation Time: 10 minutes
Cooking Time: 0 minutes
Servings: 4
Ingredients:
- 4 medium cucumbers, peeled, seeded, and chopped
- ½ cup low-fat Greek yogurt
- 1½ tablespoon fresh dill, chopped
- 1 tablespoon fresh lemon juice
- Salt and freshly ground black pepper, as required

Directions:
1. In a large bowl, add all the ingredients and mix well.
2. Serve immediately.

Nutrition:
- Calories: 71
- Carbs: 13.8 g
- Protein: 4 g
- Fat: 0.8 g
- Sugar: 7.3 g
- Sodium: 69 mg
- Fiber: 1.7 g

62. LIGHT VEGGIE SALAD

Preparation Time: 10 minutes
Cooking Time: 0 minutes
Servings: 5
Ingredients:
- 2 cups cucumbers, peeled, seeded, and chopped
- 2 cups red tomatoes, peeled, seeded, and chopped
- 2 tablespoons extra-virgin olive oil
- 2 tablespoons fresh lime juice
- Salt to taste

Directions:
1. In a large serving bowl, add all the ingredients and toss to coat well.
2. Serve immediately.

Nutrition:
- Calories: 68
- Carbs: 04.4 g
- Protein: 0.9 g
- Fat: 5.8 g
- Sugar: 2.6 g
- Sodium: 35 mg
- Fiber: 1.1 g

63. EASTERN EUROPEAN SOUP

Cooking Time: 5 minutes
Preparation Time: 10 minutes
Servings: 3
Ingredients:
- 2 cups fat-free yogurt
- 4 teaspoons fresh lemon juice
- 2 cups beets, trimmed, peeled, and chopped
- 2 tablespoons fresh dill
- Salt as required
- 1 tablespoon fresh chives, minced

Directions:
1. In a high-speed blender, add all ingredients except for chives and pulse until smooth.
2. Transfer the soup into a pan over medium heat and cook for about 3-5 minutes or until heated through.
3. Serve immediately with the garnishing of chives.

Nutrition:
- Calories: 149
- Carbs: 25.2 g
- Protein: 11.8 g
- Fat: 0.6 g
- Sugar: 21.7 g
- Sodium: 269 mg
- Fiber: 2.5 g

64. CITRUS GLAZED CARROTS
by Mildred Petersen – Cincinnati

Preparation Time: 15 minutes
Cooking Time: 15 minutes
Servings: 6

Ingredients:
- 1½ lb. carrots, peeled and sliced into ½-inch pieces diagonally
- ½ cup water
- 2 tablespoons olive oil
- Salt to taste
- 3 tablespoons fresh orange juice

Directions:
1. In a large skillet, add the carrots, water, boil, and salt over medium heat and bring to a boil.
2. Reduce heat to low and simmer; covered for about 6 minutes.
3. Add the orange juice and stir to combine.
4. Increase the heat to high and cook, uncovered for about 5-8 minutes, tossing frequently. Serve immediately.

Nutrition:
- Calories: 90
- Carbs: 12 g
- Protein: 1 g
- Fat: 4.7 g
- Sugar: 6.2 g
- Sodium: 106 mg
- Fiber: 2.8 g

65. SPRING FLAVORED PASTA
by Lena Morris – Houston

Preparation Time: 10 minutes
Cooking Time: 10 minutes
Servings: 4

Ingredients:
- 2 tablespoons olive oil
- 1 lb. asparagus, trimmed and cut into 1½-inch pieces
- Salt and freshly ground black pepper, to taste
- ½ lb. cooked hot pasta, drained

Directions:
1. In a large cast-iron skillet, heat the oil over medium heat and cook the asparagus, salt, and black pepper for about 8-10 minutes, stirring occasionally.
2. Place the hot pasta and toss to coat well.
3. Serve immediately.

Nutrition:
- Calories: 246
- Carbs: 35.2 g
- Protein: 8.9 g
- Fat: 8.4 g
- Sugar: 2.1 g
- Sodium: 17 mg
- Fiber: 2.4 g

66. GLUTEN-FREE CURRY
by Kelli Helland – Haskell

Preparation Time: 15 minutes
Cooking Time: 20 minutes
Servings: 6

Ingredients:
- 2 cups tomatoes, peeled, seeded, and chopped
- 1½ cup water
- 2 tablespoons olive oil
- 1 teaspoon fresh ginger, chopped
- ¼ teaspoon ground turmeric
- 2 cups fresh shiitake mushrooms, sliced
- 5 cups fresh button mushrooms, sliced
- ¼ cup fat-free yogurt, whipped
- Salt and freshly ground black pepper to taste

Directions:

1. In a food processor, add the tomatoes and ¼ cup of water and pulse until a smooth paste forms.
2. In a pan, heat the oil over medium heat and sauté the ginger and turmeric for about 1 minute.
3. Add the tomato paste and cook for about 5 minutes.
4. Stir in the mushrooms, yogurt, and remaining water and bring to a boil.
5. Cook for about 10-12 minutes, stirring occasionally.
6. Season with salt and black pepper and remove from the heat.
7. Serve hot.

Nutrition:
- Calories: 70
- Carbs: 5.3 g
- Protein: 3 g
- Fat: 5 g
- Sugar: 3.4 g
- Sodium: 41 mg
- Fiber: 1.4 g

Snacks

67. ALMOND PEANUT BUTTER FUDGE

Preparation Time: 2 hours 10 minutes
Cooking Time: 0 minutes
Servings: 2

Ingredients:
- 1 cup peanut butter (unsweetened)
- ¼ cup vanilla almond milk (unsweetened)
- 1 cup coconut oil
- 2 teaspoons vanilla liquid stevia (optional)
- A pinch of salt

For the Chocolate Sauce (topping):
- 2 tablespoons melted coconut oil
- 1/4 cup cocoa powder (unsweetened)
- 2 tablespoons maple syrup

Directions:

For Chocolate Sauce:
1. Take a bowl and add the coconut oil, maple syrup, and cocoa powder
2. Whisk together completely and keep it aside.

For Peanut Butter Fudge:
1. Slightly melt the coconut oil and peanut butter together over low heat on the stove (you can also use the microwave).
2. Add this melted mixture, vanilla almond milk, stevia, and salt to the blender. Blend well until thoroughly combined.
3. Pour this blended mixture into a loaf pan lined with parchment. Refrigerate for 2 hours until set.
4. Drizzle the chocolate sauce over the fudge after it has been set. Refrigerate it for some more time and then serve.

Nutrition:
- Calories: 287
- Fat: 30 g
- Carbs: 4 g
- Fiber: 2 g
- Protein: 5 g

68. QUICK COCOA MOUSSE

Preparation Time: 10 minutes

Cooking Time: 0 minutes
Servings: 8
Ingredients:
- 6 tablespoons heavy whipping cream (whip it and keep ready)
- 4 tablespoons butter (unsalted)
- 1 tablespoon cocoa powder
- 4 tablespoons cream cheese
- 1 teaspoon coconut oil
- Stevia (as per taste)

Directions:
1. Soften the butter in a microwave and then combine it with stevia. Stir well until it blends completely.
2. Add the cream cheese and cocoa powder to the butter mixture. Blend thoroughly until it becomes smooth.
3. Slowly add the whipped heavy cream to the mixture and keep stirring. Add 1 teaspoon of MCT oil or coconut oil to the mixture and blend again.
4. Spoon the smooth mixture into small glasses and refrigerate for 30 minutes. Serve chilled.

Nutrition:
- Calories: 227
- Fat: 2 g
- Carbs: 3 g
- Fiber: 1 g
- Protein: 4 g

69. CINNAMON PEAR CHIPS

Preparation Time: 5 minutes
Cooking Time: 3 hours
Servings: 4
Ingredients:
- 4 pears
- 1 teaspoon ground cinnamon

Directions:
1. Preheat the oven to 200°F. Line a baking sheet with parchment paper.
2. Core the pears and cut them into 1/8-inch slices. Toss pears with cinnamon.
3. Spread the pears in a single layer on the prepared baking sheet. Cook for 2 to 3 hours until the pears are dry.
4. They will still be soft while hot but will crisp once completely cooled. Store in an airtight container for up to four days.

Nutrition:
- Calories: 96
- Fat: 0 g
- Carbs: 26 g
- Fiber: 1 g
- Protein: 1 g

70. CHOCOLATE YOGURT CREAM & ROASTED BANANAS

Preparation Time: 10 minutes
Cooking Time: 5 minutes
Servings: 4
Ingredients:
- ½ cup whipping cream
- ½ teaspoon ground cinnamon
- 1 ½ cup low-fat vanilla yogurt (chilled and drained)
- 1 tablespoon cold butter
- 1 tablespoon confectioner's sugar
- 1 tablespoon dark rum
- 2 tablespoons unsweetened cocoa powder
- 3 tablespoons dark brown sugar
- 4 bananas (cut in strips)

Directions:
1. Place bananas cut side up on a baking sheet coated with cooking spray.
2. Sprinkle with brown sugar, rum, and cinnamon. Dot with butter.
3. Roast in a 425°F preheated oven for five minutes. Turn the broiler off until the bananas are golden.
4. Meanwhile, beat the cocoa, cream, and confectioner's sugar in a large bowl using an electric mixer.
5. Add the drained yogurt and fold the cream until well combined. Plate the roasted bananas and add a dollop of chocolate cream on top.

Nutrition:
- Calories: 236
- Fat: 0 g
- Carbs: 42 g
- Fiber: 3 g
- Protein: 7 g

71. COCONUT CELERY SMOOTHIE

Preparation Time: 10 minutes

Cooking Time: 0 minutes
Servings: 2
Ingredients:
- 3 celery stalks (shredded)
- 1 teaspoon ground cinnamon
- ½ banana
- 1 scoop protein powder
- 1 tablespoon coconut butter
- 1 cup unsweetened coconut milk

Directions:
1. Toss your ingredients into a blender, then process until creamy and smooth. Serve immediately and enjoy.

Nutrition:
- Calories: 391
- Fat: 15 g
- Carbs: 42 g
- Fiber: 1 g
- Protein: 29 g

72. APPLE SPINACH SMOOTHIE

Preparation Time: 10 minutes
Cooking Time: 0 minutes
Servings: 2
Ingredients:
- ¼ teaspoon vanilla extract
- 1 teaspoon ginger (grated)
- 1 teaspoon maple syrup
- 1 ½ tablespoon coconut butter
- ½ cup yogurt
- 1 apple (chopped)
- 1 cup baby spinach
- 1 cup unsweetened coconut milk

Directions:
1. Toss your ingredients into a blender, then process until creamy and smooth. Serve immediately and enjoy.

Nutrition:
- Calories: 388
- Fat: 19 g
- Carbs: 43 g
- Fiber: 3 g
- Protein: 15 g

73. BANANA COCOA CREAM

Preparation Time: 4 hours
Cooking Time: 0 minutes
Servings: 4
Ingredients:
- 1 banana (mashed)
- Cocoa powder to taste
- Stevia to taste (optional)

Directions:
1. Mix one mashed banana with stevia and cocoa powder. You may blend these together or use a food processor for best results.
2. Freeze in a sealed container for 2-4 hours.

Nutrition:
- Calories: 0.1
- Fat: 1 g
- Carbs: 7 g
- Fiber: 1 g
- Protein: 0 g

74. HOMEMADE PUMPKIN PIE
by Jill T. Greenhill - Naperville

Preparation Time: 5 minutes.
Servings: 10
Cooking Time: 45 minutes.

Ingredients:

Crust:
- 1 half-batch All-Butter Pie crust, fitted into a 9-inch, crimped and chilled

Filling:
- 1 15-ounce can pumpkin purée
- ¾ cup sugar
- 2 large eggs (at room temperature)
- 11 oz. lactose-free evaporated milk
- 1 teaspoon cinnamon
- ½ teaspoon ginger (ground)
- 1/4 teaspoon salt
- ¼ teaspoon cloves (ground)

Directions:
1. Position rack in center of oven. Set oven to preheat to 425°F. Whisk eggs, sugar, and pumpkin together in a medium bowl.

2. Whisk in your salt, cinnamon, ginger, clove, and evaporated milk until smooth.

3. Add filling to your crust and set to bake for 15 minutes. Turn heat down to 350°F (180°C) and continue to bake until filling is set, about 35 to 45 minutes.

4. Cool completely, then serve. Pie is best served the day it is baked, but it can be made 1 day ahead; store at room temperature, lightly covered with foil.

Nutrition:
- Calories: 342
- Fat: 1 g
- Carbs: 42 g
- Fiber: 1 g
- Protein: 5 g

75. ZERO SUGAR PUMPKIN PIE
by Lorraine Greenwood - Gonzales

Preparation Time: 10 minutes
Cooking Time: 1 hour
Servings: 16

Ingredients:
- 1 15-ounce can pumpkin
- 3/4 teaspoon ground cinnamon
- 1/2 teaspoon ground nutmeg
- 1/2 teaspoon ground ginger
- 1/2 teaspoon ground cloves
- 1 14-ounce can evaporated skim milk
- 2 large eggs (slightly beaten)
- 1/2 cup Splenda
- 9" deep dish pie crust (refined white flour)

Directions:
1. Baked at 350°F for 1 hour. Makes 16 small servings.

Nutrition:
- Calories: 84
- Fat: 3 g
- Carbs: 1 g
- Fiber: 3 g
- Protein: 35 g

76. ORANGE CURD
by Sheila C. Smith San Francisco

Preparation Time: 5 minutes
Cooking Time: 15 minutes
Servings: 20

Ingredients:
- 55 g butter
- 225 g sugar
- 2 large eggs (beaten)
- Juice and finely grated zest of 2 oranges

Directions:
2. Put a bowl over a pan of simmering water and add the butter and sugar until dissolved. Add the orange zest and juice.

3. Gently whisk while adding the eggs. Let it cook gently stirring until it is thick, and like custard. This should take 15 minutes. Remove it from the heat and place it in a jar.

Nutrition:
- Calories: 72
- Fat: 3 g
- Carbs: 12 g
- Fiber: 1 g
- Protein: 1 g

77. INSTANT POT PEAR CRUMBLE
by Barbara Moran - Scottsdale

Preparation Time: 15 minutes
Cooking Time: 25 minutes
Servings: 6

Ingredients:
- 5 large pears (cut into 1-inch chunks)
- 1/3 cup water
- 3 Tablespoons flour
- ¾ cup quick oats
- ½ cup coconut sugar
- 2 teaspoons ground cinnamon
- ¼ teaspoon fine sea salt
- ¼ cup melted coconut oil or butter

Directions:
1. Add your water and pears into your Instant Pot and stir well to be sure the pears cover the bottom of the pot in an even layer.

2. In a separate bowl, combine salt, cinnamon, sugar, oats, and flour, then stir well.

3. Add the melted coconut oil and stir until thoroughly mixed. Top pears with crumble.

4. Select Manual/Pressure. Cook on high pressure for 8 minutes. Naturally, release the pressure from your IP (about 10 minutes).

5. Remove the lid. Use oven mitts to remove the dish from the Instant Pot and let the crumble cool for 10 minutes before serving warm.

Nutrition:
- Calories: 279
- Fat: 10 g
- Carbs: 48 g
- Fiber: 1 g
- Protein: 2 g

Dinner

78. CHICKEN CUTLETS

Preparation Time: 10 minutes
Cooking Time: 15 minutes
Servings: 4
Ingredients:
- 4 teaspoons red wine vinegar
- 2 teaspoons minced garlic cloves
- 2 teaspoons dried sage leaves
- 1 lb. chicken breast cutlets
- Salt and pepper to taste
- 1/4 cup refined white flour
- 2 teaspoons olive oil

Directions:

1. Set a good amount of plastic wrap on the kitchen counter; sprinkle with half the combined sage, garlic, and vinegar.

2. Put the chicken breast on the plastic wrap; sprinkle with the rest of the vinegar mixture. Season lightly with pepper and salt.

3. Secure the chicken with the second sheet of plastic wrap. Use a kitchen mallet to pound the breast until it is flattened. Let stand 5 minutes.

4. Set the chicken on both sides with flour. In a skillet, heat the oil over medium heat.

5. Add half of the chicken breast and cook for 1 ½ minute or until it is browned on the bottom.

6. Turn on the other side and let it cook for 3 minutes.

7. Remove the chicken breast and place it on an oven-proof serving plate so that you can keep warm.

8. Reduce the liquid by half. Pour the mixture over the chicken breast; serve immediately.

Nutrition:
- Calories: 549
- Fat: 6 g
- Carbs: 7 g
- Fiber: 1 g
- Protein: 114 g

79. SLOW COOKER SALSA TURKEY

Preparation Time: 8 minutes
Cooking Time: 7 hours

Servings: 4
Ingredients:
- 2 lbs. turkey breasts, boneless and skinless
- 1 cup salsa
- 1 cup small tomatoes, diced, canned choose low-sodium
- 2 tablespoons taco seasoning
- 1/2 cup celery, finely diced
- 1/2 cup carrots, shredded
- 3 tablespoons low-fat sour cream
- ½ cup water

Directions:
1. Add the turkey to your slow cooker. Season it with taco seasoning, then top with salsa and vegetables.
2. Add in 1/2 cup of water. Set to cook on low for 7 hours (internal temperature should be 165°F when done).
3. Shred the turkey with 2 forks, add in sour cream, and stir. Enjoy.

Nutrition:
- Calories: 178
- Fat: 4 g
- Carbs: 7 g
- Fiber: 2 g
- Protein: 27 g

80. SRIRACHA LIME CHICKEN AND APPLE SALAD

Preparation Time: 10 minutes
Cooking Time: 15 minutes
Servings: 4
Ingredients:

Sriracha Lime Chicken:
- 2 organic chicken breasts
- 3 tablespoons sriracha
- 1 lime, juiced
- 1/4 teaspoon fine sea salt
- 1/4 teaspoon freshly ground pepper

Fruit Salad:
- 4 apples, peeled, cored, and diced
- 1 cup organic grape tomatoes
- 1/3 cup red onion, finely chopped

Lime Vinaigrette:
- 1/3 cup light olive oil
- 1/4 cup apple cider vinegar
- 2 limes, juiced
- A dash of fine sea salt

Directions:
1. Use salt and pepper to season the chicken on both sides. Spread on the sriracha and lime and let sit for 20 minutes.
2. Cook the chicken per side over medium heat or until done. Grill the apple with the chicken.
3. Meanwhile, whisk together the dressing and season to taste.
4. Arrange the salad, topping it with red onion and tomatoes.
5. Serve as a side to the chicken and apple.

Nutrition:
- Calories: 484
- Fat: 28 g
- Carbs: 32 g
- Fiber: 8 g
- Protein: 30 g

81. PAN-SEARED SCALLOPS WITH LEMON-GINGER VINAIGRETTE

Preparation Time: 10 minutes
Cooking Time: 10 minutes
Servings: 2
Ingredients:
- 1 lb. sea scallops
- 1 tablespoon extra-virgin olive oil
- 1/4 teaspoon sea salt
- 2 tablespoons lemon-ginger vinaigrette
- A pinch of freshly ground black pepper

Directions:
1. Heat the olive oil in a non-stick skillet or pan over medium-high heat until it starts shimmering.
2. Add the scallops to the skillet or pan after seasoning them with pepper and salt. Cook for 3 minutes per side or until the fish is only opaque.
3. Serve with a dollop of vinaigrette on top.

Nutrition:
- Calories: 280
- Fat: 16
- Carbs: 5 g
- Sugar: 1 g

- Fiber: 0 g
- Protein: 29 g
- Sodium: 508 mg

82. ROASTED SALMON AND ASPARAGUS

Preparation Time: 5 minutes
Cooking Time: 15 minutes
Servings: 2

Ingredients:
- 1 tablespoon extra-virgin olive oil
- 1 pound salmon, cut into two fillets
- 1/2 lemon zest and slices
- 1/2 pound asparagus spears, trimmed
- 1 teaspoon sea salt, divided
- 1/8 teaspoon freshly cracked black pepper

Directions:
1. Preheat the oven to 425°F.
2. Stir the asparagus with half of salt and olive oil. At the base of a roasting tray, spread in a continuous sheet.
3. Season the salmon with salt and pepper. Place the asparagus on top of the skin-side down.
4. Lemon zest should be sprinkled over the asparagus, salmon, and lemon slices. Set them over the top.
5. Roast for around 15 minutes until the flesh of the fish is opaque in the preheated oven.

Nutrition:
- Calories: 308
- Fat: 18 g
- Carbs: 5 g
- Sugar: 2 g
- Fiber: 2 g
- Protein: 36 g
- Sodium: 542 mg

83. COD WITH GINGER AND BLACK BEANS

Preparation Time: 10 minutes
Cooking Time: 15 minutes
Servings: 2

Ingredients:
- 2 (6 oz.) cod fillets
- 1/2 teaspoon sea salt, divided
- 3 minced garlic cloves
- 2 tablespoons chopped fresh cilantro leaves
- 1 tablespoon extra-virgin olive oil
- 1/2 tablespoon grated fresh ginger
- 2 tablespoons freshly ground black pepper
- 1/2 (14 oz.) can black beans, drained

Directions:
1. Heat the olive oil in a big non-stick skillet or pan over medium-high heat until it starts shimmering.
2. Half of the salt, ginger, and pepper are used to season the fish. Cook for around 4 minutes per side in the hot oil until the fish is opaque. Remove the cod from the pan and place it on a plate with aluminum foil tented over it.
3. Add the garlic to the skillet or pan and return it to the heat. Cook for 30 seconds while continuously stirring.
4. Mix the black beans and the remaining salt. Cook, stirring regularly, for 5 minutes.
5. Add the cilantro and serve the black beans on top of the cod.

Nutrition:
- Calories: 419
- Fat: 2 g
- Carbs: 33 g
- Sugar: 1 g
- Fiber: 8 g
- Protein: 50 g
- Sodium: 605 mg

84. HALIBUT CURRY

Preparation Time: 10 minutes
Cooking Time: 10 minutes
Servings: 2

Ingredients:
- 1 teaspoon ground turmeric
- 1 lb. halibut, skin, and bones removed, cut into 1-inch pieces
- 1/2 (14 oz.) can coconut milk
- 1/8 teaspoon ground black pepper
- 1 tablespoon extra-virgin olive oil
- 1 teaspoon curry powder
- 2 cups no-salt-added chicken broth
- 1/4 teaspoon sea salt

Directions:
1. Heat the olive oil in a non-stick skillet or pan over medium-high heat until it starts shimmering.

2. Add the curry powder and turmeric to a bowl. To bloom the spices, cook for 2 minutes, stirring continuously.

3. Stir in the halibut, coconut milk, chicken broth, pepper, and salt. Lower the heat to medium-low and bring to a simmer. Cook, stirring regularly, for 6-7 minutes, or until the fish is opaque.

Nutrition:
- Calories: 429
- Fat: 47 g
- Carbs: 5 g
- Sugar: 1 g
- Fiber: 1 g
- Protein: 27 g
- Sodium: 507 mg

85. CHICKEN CACCIATORE
by Ruby Murphy – Quitman

Preparation Time: 10 minutes
Cooking Time: 20 minutes
Servings: 2

Ingredients:
- 1 lb. skinless chicken, cut into bite-size pieces
- 1/4 cup black olives, chopped
- 1/2 teaspoon onion powder
- A pinch of freshly ground black pepper
- 1 tablespoon extra-virgin olive oil
- 1 (28 oz.) can crushed tomatoes, drained
- 1/2 teaspoon garlic powder
- 1/4 teaspoon sea salt

Directions:
1. Heat the olive oil in a non-stick skillet or pan over medium-high heat until it starts shimmering.
2. Cook until the chicken is browned.
3. Add the tomatoes, garlic powder, olives, salt, onion powder, and pepper, then stir to combine. Cook, stirring regularly, for 10 minutes.

Nutrition:
- Calories: 305
- Fat: 11 g
- Carbs: 34 g
- Sugar: 23 g
- Fiber: 13 g
- Protein: 19 g
- Sodium: 1.171 mg

86. CHICKEN AND BELL PEPPER SAUTE'
by Linda Rueda – Owatonna

Preparation Time: 5 minutes
Cooking Time: 15 minutes
Servings: 2

Ingredients:
- 1 chopped bell pepper
- 1 lb. skinless chicken breasts, cut into bite-size pieces
- 1 ½ tablespoon extra-virgin olive oil
- 1/2 chopped onion
- 3 minced garlic cloves
- 1/8 teaspoon ground black pepper
- 1/4 teaspoon sea salt

Directions:
1. Heat the olive oil in a non-stick skillet or pan over medium-high heat until it starts shimmering.
2. Add the onion, red bell pepper, and chicken. Cook, stirring regularly, for 10 minutes.
3. Stir in the salt, garlic, and pepper in a mixing bowl. Cook for 30 seconds while continuously stirring.

Nutrition:
- Calories: 179
- Fat: 13 g
- Carbs: 6 g
- Sugar: 3 g
- Fiber: 1 g
- Protein: 10 g
- Sodium: 265 mg

87. CHICKEN SALAD SANDWICHES
by Florence Washington – St Peters

Preparation Time: 15 minutes
Cooking Time: 0 minutes
Servings: 2

Ingredients:
- 2 tablespoons anti-inflammatory mayonnaise
- 1 tablespoon chopped fresh tarragon leaves
- 1 cup chicken, chopped, cooked, and skinless (from 1 rotisserie chicken)

- 1/2 minced red bell pepper
- 1 teaspoon Dijon mustard
- 4 slices whole-wheat bread
- 1/4 teaspoon sea salt

Directions:

1. Combine the chicken, red bell pepper, mayonnaise, mustard, tarragon, and salt in a medium mixing bowl.
2. Spread on 2 pieces of bread and top it with the remaining bread.

Nutrition:
- Calories: 315
- Fat: 9 g
- Carbs: 30 g
- Sugar: 6 g
- Fiber: 4 g
- Protein: 28 g
- Sodium: 677 mg

88. ROSEMARY CHICKEN
by Robin Pulver – Nashville

Preparation Time: 15 minutes
Cooking Time: 20 minutes
Servings: 2

Ingredients:
- 1 tablespoon extra-virgin olive oil
- 1 lb. chicken breast tenders
- 1 tablespoon chopped fresh rosemary leaves
- 1/8 teaspoon ground black pepper
- 1/4 teaspoon sea salt

Directions:

1. Preheat the oven to 425°F.
2. Set the chicken tenders on a baking sheet with a rim. Sprinkle with salt, rosemary, and pepper after brushing them with olive oil.
3. For 15-20 minutes, keep in the oven, just before the juices run clear.

Nutrition:
- Calories: 389
- Fat: 20 g
- Carbs: 1 g
- Sugar: 0 g
- Fiber: 1 g
- Protein: 49 g
- Sodium: 381 mg

Dessert

89. PAPAYA-MANGO SMOOTHIE

Preparation Time: 5 minutes
Cooking Time: 0 minutes
Servings: 2
Ingredients:
- 1 cup mango, diced
- 1 cup papaya chunks
- 1 cup almond or lactose-free milk
- 1 tablespoon honey or maple syrup

Directions:
1. Blend all ingredients in a blender and then pulse until smooth.
2. Pour into a large glass. Enjoy!

Nutrition:
- Calories: 554
- Fat: 32 g
- Carbs: 14 g
- Sugar: 8 g
- Fiber: 2 g
- Protein: 50 g
- Sodium: 632 mg

90. CANTALOUPE SMOOTHIE

Preparation Time: 5 minutes
Cooking Time: 0 minutes
Servings: 2
Ingredients:
- 1 cup cantaloupe, diced
- 1/2 cup vanilla yogurt or lactose-free yogurt
- 1/2 cup orange juice
- 1 tablespoon honey or maple syrup
- 2 ice cubes

Directions:
1. Merge all ingredients in a blender and then pulse until smooth.
2. Pour into a large glass. Enjoy!

Nutrition:
- Calories: 179
- Fat: 13 g
- Carbs: 6 g
- Sugar: 3 g
- Fiber: 1 g
- Protein: 10 g
- Sodium: 265 mg

91. CANTALOUPE-MIX SMOOTHIE

Preparation Time: 5-10 minutes
Cooking Time: 0 minutes
Servings: 2
Ingredients:
- 1 cup cantaloupe, diced
- 1/2 cup mango, diced
- 1/2 cup almond milk or lactose-free cow milk
- 1/2 cup orange juice
- 2 tablespoons lemon
- 1 tablespoon honey or maple syrup
- 2 ice cubes

Directions:
1. Merge all ingredients in a blender until smooth.
2. Pour into a large glass. Enjoy!

Nutrition:
- Calories: 329
- Fat: 17 g
- Carbs: 9 g
- Sugar: 3 g
- Fiber: 5 g
- Protein: 37 g
- Sodium: 430 mg

92. APPLESAUCE-AVOCADO SMOOTHIE

Preparation Time: 5-10 minutes
Cooking Time: 0 minutes
Servings: 1
Ingredients:
- 1 cup unsweetened almond or lactose-free milk
- 1/2 avocado
- 1/2 cup applesauce
- 1/4 teaspoon ground cinnamon
- 1/2 cup ice

- 1/2 teaspoon stevia or 1 tablespoon honey for sweetness (optional)

Directions:
1. Blend all ingredients in a blender. Pulse the mix until smooth.
2. Pour into a large glass. Enjoy!

Nutrition:
- Calories: 270
- Fat: 11 g
- Carbs: 4 g
- Sugar: 1 g
- Fiber: 1 g
- Protein: 39 g
- Sodium: 664 mg

93. PINA COLADA SMOOTHIE

Preparation Time: 5-10 minutes
Cooking Time: 0 minutes
Servings: 1

Ingredients:
- 1 cup papaya chunks
- 1/2 cup unsweetened almond milk or lactose-free milk
- 1 banana
- 1/2 teaspoon vanilla extract, to taste
- 1 tablespoon honey, maple syrup or 1 teaspoon stevia (optional)

Directions:
1. Blend all ingredients in a blender and then pulse until smooth and creamy.
2. Pour into a large glass. Enjoy!

Nutrition:
- Calories: 329
- Fat: 17 g
- Carbs: 9 g
- Sugar: 3 g
- Fiber: 5 g
- Protein: 37 g
- Sodium: 430 mg

94. DICED FRUITS

Preparation Time: 10 minutes
Cooking Time: 40 minutes
Servings: 6

Ingredients:
- 4 peaches, skin removed and thinly sliced
- 1 lb. apple, pitted and skin removed
- 1 teaspoon cinnamon powder
- 1 cup honey or maple syrup
- 1 teaspoon vanilla extract

Directions:
1. In a large pot, cook the fruits in boiling water over medium heat until softened.
2. In a large bowl, mix well all ingredients (except the fruits).
3. Pour the syrup over fruits and let the compote be thickened.
4. Pour the compote into a jar. Serve hot or cold. Enjoy!

Nutrition:
- Calories: 178
- Fat: 4 g
- Carbs: 7 g
- Fiber: 2 g
- Protein: 27 g

95. APPLESAUCE

Preparation Time: 10 minutes
Cooking Time: 30 minutes
Servings: 4

Ingredients:
- 6 organic apples, peeled, cored, and cubed
- 1/2 cup boiling water
- 1/2 teaspoon cinnamon powder
- 1/4 cup sugar or 4 tablespoons honey
- 2 tablespoons fresh lemon juice
- 1/4 teaspoon salt

Directions:
1. In a large pot, cook apples with boiling water, lemon juice, cinnamon, sugar, or honey, and salt over medium-low heat until softened. Remove from the heat.
2. You can mash all ingredients by using a fork or blend with a blender or a food processor.
3. Pour the applesauce into a suitable container or jar. Serve warm or cold. Enjoy!

Nutrition:

- Calories: 51
- Fat: 3 g
- Carbs: 4 g
- Fiber: 2 g
- Protein: 2 g

96. AVOCADO DIP
by Inez T. Howes – Annapolis Junction

Preparation Time: 10 minutes
Cooking Time: 0 minutes
Servings: 4

Ingredients:
- 6 avocados, peeled
- 1/2 tablespoon extra-virgin olive oil
- 1/4 cup chopped fresh cilantro
- 2 tablespoons fresh lime juice
- 1 teaspoon fresh lemon juice
- 1/2 teaspoon salt

Directions:
1. In a large bowl, set avocados with a fork.
2. Add extra-virgin olive oil and the other ingredients. Enjoy!

Nutrition:
- Calories: 75
- Carbs: 0.1 g
- Protein: 13.4 g
- Fat: 1.7 g
- Sugar: 0 g
- Sodium: 253 mg

97. HOMEMADE HUMMUS
by Gonzalo Richardson – Mccook

Preparation Time: 10 minutes
Cooking Time: 60 minutes
Servings: 4

Ingredients:
- 1/4 lb. dried chickpeas (soaked in water for a night)
- 11/2 tablespoon tahini
- 1 tablespoon lemon juice
- 2 tablespoons extra-virgin olive oil, divided
- 1/4 teaspoon cumin powder
- 1/2 teaspoon salt
- 1 tablespoon water
- 1 teaspoon baking soda (optional)
- 1 teaspoon paprika powder (optional)

Directions:
1. First, you need to soak the chickpeas overnight in water, and optionally, add baking soda to the water.
2. Cook your chickpeas in a large pot with water over medium heat for about 1 hour. Check if they are cooked well by crushing one of them with a fork in your hand.
3. When chickpeas are cooked, drain and put them in a blender.
4. Add 1 tablespoon of extra-virgin olive oil, lemon juice, tahini, cumin powder, and salt to the blender. Blend until your hummus gets a soft, creamy texture equally.
5. Drizzle with 1 tablespoon of extra-virgin olive oil or paprika powder (optional).
6. Serve immediately or fridge it.

Nutrition:
- Calories: 207
- Fat: 16 g
- Carbs: 5 g
- Sugar: 2 g
- Fiber: 1 g
- Protein: 12 g
- Sodium: 366 mg

98. TOFU
by Martha Hale – Brevard

Preparation Time: 10 minutes
Cooking Time: 25 minutes
Servings: 4

Ingredients:
- 1 ½ cup firm tofu, pressed and drained
- 1 avocado, cubed
- 1 tablespoon extra-virgin olive oil
- Salt and pepper to taste

Directions:
1. Preheat your oven to 400°F.
2. Choose a baking sheet, cover it with parchment paper or spray extra-virgin olive oil. Cut tofu cubes of 1/2 inch and spray extra-virgin olive oil on them.

3. Let it bake for 15 minutes until golden brown and crispy. Flip tofu and cook for another 10 minutes. Remove from the oven. Let it rest for 10 minutes.
4. Cube the avocado on a plate. Add salt and pepper.
5. Mix the tofu with avocado in a bowl. Enjoy!

Nutrition:
- Calories: 645
- Fat: 32 g
- Carbs: 65 g
- Fiber: 5 g
- Protein: 26 g

CHAPTER 6
HIGH-FIBER DIET

BE PART OF THIS COMMUNITY OF CRAZY INNOVATORS AND
SHARE YOUR UNCONVENTIONAL KNOWLEDGE...BE PART OF ...
FUN CLUB KITCHEN

Breakfast

99. PEAR TURKEY PITA

Preparation Time: 15 minutes
Cooking Time: 0 minutes
Servings: 4
Ingredients:
- 2 cups turkey (cooked, cubed)
- 2 medium pears (unpeeled, chopped)
- 1 stalk celery (chopped)
- 1/3 cup yogurt (plain, low-fat, or non-fat)
- 1/4 cup mayonnaise (non-fat)
- 4 pita bread (round, whole wheat)
- 4 lettuce leaves (romaine)
- Mixed fruits for serving

Directions:
1. In a bowl, combine the turkey, celery, and pears. Add mayonnaise and yogurt, then combine. Create a pocket by slicing the pita.
2. Put the lettuce leaf inside the pita and fill the pocket with 1 cup of mixture in each pita bread.
3. Serve with mixed fruits. (Do not include berries.)

Nutrition:
- Calories: 221
- Fat: 3 g
- Carbs: 21 g
- Fiber: 2 g
- Protein: 25 g

100. OVERNIGHT OATS

Preparation Time: 5 minutes
Cooking Time: 0 minutes
Servings: 4
Ingredients:
- 1 cup almond milk
- 1/2 cup fruit of choice
- 1 cup gluten-free oats
- ½ tablespoon honey

Directions:
1. Mix 1 cup oats with 2/3 cup almond milk. Add fruit and honey.
2. Leave in refrigerator overnight in a Mason jar or a similarly sealable container. Mix well in the morning before eating.

Nutrition:
- Calories: 267
- Fat: 16 g
- Carbs: 34 g
- Fiber: 4 g
- Protein: 4 g

101. VEGGIE SCRAMBLE

Preparation Time: 5 minutes
Cooking Time: 0 minutes
Servings: 1
Ingredients:
- 2 eggs
- 1 cup spinach
- 1 medium tomato
- Cooking spray

Directions:
1. Mix eggs, spinach, and chopped tomato in a bowl.
2. Spray a pan with cooking spray and pour bowl contents onto the pan when hot. Cook until eggs are no longer runny.

Nutrition:
- Calories: 157
- Fat: 6 g
- Carbs: 15 g
- Fiber: 6 g
- Protein: 16 g

102. TURKEY AND AVOCADO PITAS

Preparation Time: 10 minutes
Cooking Time: 0 minutes
Servings: 4
Ingredients:
- 2 cups turkey (cooked, cubed)
- 1 medium avocado (chopped)
- 1 (14-ounce) can of red beans (drained and rinsed)
- 1 teaspoon lemon juice
- 1 cup tomatoes (seeded, chopped)
- 1 cup low-fat cottage cheese

- 4 round whole wheat pita bread

Directions:
1. In a large mixing bowl, combine turkey, avocado, red beans, lemon juice, tomatoes, and cottage cheese.
2. Slice the pita bread to make a pocket and spoon in the turkey mixture. Serve.

Nutrition:
- Calories: 277
- Fat: 11 g
- Carbs: 10 g
- Fiber: 4 g
- Protein: 30 g

103. GRILLED VEGETABLE SANDWICH

Preparation Time: 10 minutes
Cooking Time: 12 minutes
Servings: 4
Ingredients:
- 1 Japanese eggplant (sliced in half-inch-thick slices)
- 1 zucchini (small, sliced in half-inch-thick slices)
- 1 red pepper (seeded and quartered)
- 2 Portobello mushroom caps
- 1/2 cup extra-virgin olive oil
- 1/4 teaspoon salt
- 6 oz. goat cheese
- 8 slices whole wheat
- 1 cup baby spinach

Directions:
1. With a pastry brush, brush olive oil on the vegetable slices and the mushrooms caps.
2. Season them with salt. Put the vegetables on the grill and cook them until they are tender.
3. To assemble, slice the mushrooms, spread goat cheese on both sides of the bread.
4. Add the grilled vegetables of each variation and a quarter of the mushrooms.
5. Cover with spinach and top with bread before serving.

Nutrition:
- Calories: 681
- Fat: 66 g
- Carbs: 14 g
- Fiber: 6 g
- Protein: 16 g

104. SPINACH AND HAM PIZZA

Preparation Time: 10 minutes
Cooking Time: 12 minutes
Servings: 4
Ingredients:
- 1 store-bought baked thin-crust whole wheat pizza shell
- 4 cups baby spinach leaves (thinly sliced)
- 2 teaspoons olive oil
- 3 oz. ham (thinly sliced)
- ¼ feta cheese (crumbled)
- 1/4 cup Parmesan cheese (grated)
- 3 garlic cloves (thinly sliced)

Directions:
1. Preheat oven to 450°F degrees. Place the pizza shell on a cookie sheet.
2. Scatter spinach all over the crust. Drizzle with oil. Place ham, garlic, and cheeses on top of spinach.
3. Bake for 10-12 minutes until the spinach is wilted.

Nutrition:
- Calories: 256
- Fat: 19 g
- Carbs: 4 g
- Fiber: 1 g
- Protein: 18 g

105. FRUIT BOWL

Preparation Time: 5 minutes
Cooking Time: 0 minutes
Servings: 4
Ingredients:
- 1 cup pears (cut in half-inch cubes)
- 1 cup bananas (cut in half-inch cubes)
- 1 cup oranges (cut in half-inch cubes)

Directions:
1. Mix all ingredients together and serve with a salad dressing.

Nutrition:
- Calories: 308

- Fat: 1 g
- Carbs: 79 g
- Fiber: 13 g
- Protein: 4 g

106. EASY TOFU & BEANS
by Bennie Lepage – Jackson

Preparation Time: 15 minutes
Cooking Time: 20 minutes
Servings: 4

Ingredients:
- 1 (14 oz) pkg. firm tofu (drained, cut into cubes)
- 1/4 cup whole wheat flour
- 1 tablespoon canola oil
- 1/2 cup olive oil
- 2 tablespoons balsamic vinegar
- 1 tablespoon Dijon mustard
- 3 tablespoons soy sauce
- 1/2 cup onions (sliced)
- 1/2 cups carrots (sliced)
- 1 cup green beans (ends cut)
- 1/2 cup fresh soybeans
- 1 1/2 cup cabbage (chopped)
- 1 cup brown rice (cooked)

Directions:
2. In a shallow bowl or plate, mix tofu with flour until evenly coated. Heat up the canola oil over medium heat in a non-stick pan.
3. Add tofu and cook until lightly brown. Remove from pan and put aside.
4. Prepare the dressing by whisking together olive oil, vinegar, mustard, and soy sauce.
5. In the same pan, combine 2 tablespoons of the dressing mixture with onions, carrots, green beans, soybeans, and cabbage.
6. Stir fry for 10 minutes. Add remaining dressing mixture and tofu. Mix. Cook for 2 minutes, stirring gently.
7. Serve over hot brown rice.

Nutrition:
- Calories: 678
- Fat: 44 g
- Carbs: 55 g
- Fiber: 6 g
- Protein: 19 g

107. COUSCOUS WITH DATES
by Michael Martinez – Kalaheo

Preparation Time: 10 minutes
Cooking Time: 10 minutes
Servings: 4

Ingredients:
- 1/2 cup water
- 1 cup turkey stock
- 1 tablespoon olive oil
- 1/2 cup dried dates (chopped)
- 1 cup couscous
- 1 cup spinach (chopped)
- 1/2 teaspoon lemon juice
- 1/2 teaspoon salt

Directions:
1. In a medium saucepan, over high heat, bring water, turkey stock, oil, and dates to a boil. Remove from heat and stir in couscous.
2. Cover and let sit for 5-10 minutes. Stir in spinach into couscous. Add lemon juice and salt and fluff together with a fork. Serve.

Nutrition:
- Calories: 197
- Fat: 4 g
- Carbs: 33 g
- Fiber: 2 g
- Protein: 6 g

108. BEAN & VEGETABLE PASTA
by Rebecca J. Carter – Albert Lea

Preparation Time: 10 minutes
Cooking Time: 26 minutes
Servings: 4

Ingredients:
- 1 lb. whole wheat penne pasta
- 2 tablespoons olive oil
- 2 garlic cloves (minced)
- 3 cups tomatoes (seeded and chopped)
- 1 (14 oz) can cannellini beans (drained and rinsed)
- 1 cup tomato sauce

- 2 cups spinach (washed and chopped)
- ½ cup crumbled feta cheese

Directions:

1. Bring salted water to boil in a pot. Add the pasta, then ensure to follow the cooking instructions on the package. Then drain it.
2. Set your oil to get hot on medium heat in a nonstick pan. Cook garlic for 3-4 minutes. Add tomatoes, beans, and tomato sauce.
3. Bring to a boil. Reduce the heat, cover, and let simmer for 10 minutes. Add spinach to the sauce and let simmer for another 5 minutes or until spinach wilts.
4. Transfer to a large bowl. Combine with your sauce, then top with feta. Toss to combine. Serve.

Nutrition:
- Calories: 232
- Fat: 16 g
- Carbs: 17 g
- Fiber: 3 g
- Protein: 17 g

Lunch

109. PORK AND PENNE PASTA

Preparation Time: 20 minutes
Cooking Time: 30 minutes
Servings: 4

Ingredients:
- 1 lb. whole wheat penne pasta
- 1 lb. ground Pork lean
- 2 tablespoons extra virgin olive oil
- 1 small onion (chopped)
- 2 garlic cloves (minced)
- 1 (15-ounce) can tomatoes (diced, seeded)
- 2 cups green zucchini (sliced to 1/4 cubes)
- 8 oz. baby spinach (fresh, chopped)
- 1 cup low-fat parmesan cheese (grated)

Directions:

1. Bring a pot of water to a boil, ensure that the water is salted. Cook the pasta to an al dente consistency or according to package directions.
2. In a non-stick pan, cook the ground pork over medium heat for 8 minutes or until it is browned. Ensure to break up any large pieces in the pan.
3. Remove pork and set aside. Discard drippings. Add in your oil on medium heat.
4. Cook onions and garlic for about 5 minutes or until soft. Add tomatoes and zucchini and continue cooking for 5 minutes more.
5. Add spinach and cook until it just wilts, 2-3 minutes. Place the pork back into the skillet and add 1/2 cup cheese; stir and heat through.
6. Plate your pasta, then top with your meat mixture. Toss well and top evenly with cheese.

Nutrition:
- Calories: 206
- Fat: 9 g
- Carbs: 24 g
- Fiber: 13 g
- Protein: 17 g

110. CHICKEN AND QUINOA PITA

Preparation Time: 10 minutes
Cooking Time: 0 minutes

Servings: 4

Ingredients:
- 1 cup fat-free cream cheese (softened)
- 1 tablespoon fat-free mayonnaise
- 2 cups cooked chicken (cubed)
- 1 cup tomatoes (seeded, sliced)
- 1 (14-ounce) can quinoa (cooked)
- 4 romaine lettuce leaves
- 2 cups alfalfa sprouts (rinsed, drained)
- 4 round whole wheat pita bread

Directions:
1. In a bowl, combine mayonnaise and cream cheese until it is fully mixed.
2. Add chicken, tomatoes, quinoa; mix well. Slice the pita bread to form a pocket.
3. Fill your pitas with lettuce and chicken. Top with alfalfa sprouts. Serve.

Nutrition:
- Calories: 331
- Fat: 23 g
- Carbs: 5 g
- Fiber: 2 g
- Protein: 26 g

111. CHICKEN AND ASPARAGUS PASTA

Preparation Time: 10 minutes
Cooking Time: 22 minutes
Servings: 4

Ingredients:
- 1 lb. whole wheat penne pasta
- 2 tablespoons olive oil
- 3/4 lb. chicken breast halves (sliced into strips)
- 1/2 teaspoon poultry seasoning
- 4 garlic cloves (minced)
- 1 1/2 cup asparagus (frozen, cut into 1 inch)
- 1 cup peas (frozen, thawed)
- 1/4 cup parmesan cheese (grated)

Directions:
1. Bring a pot of salted water to boil. Add pasta and cook to an al dente consistency according to package directions.
2. Heat one tablespoon olive oil in a non-stick pan over medium heat and cook chicken with poultry seasoning until golden.
3. Remove cooked chicken from the pan.
4. Add the remaining tablespoon of olive oil, garlic, asparagus, and peas. Cook until vegetables are tender.
5. Put the chicken back into the pan with the asparagus mixture and cook for 2 minutes.
6. Put the pasta in a shallow pasta bowl and toss with chicken mixture. Top with parmesan cheese.

Nutrition:
- Calories: 168
- Fat: 10 g
- Carbs: 7 g
- Fiber: 3 g
- Protein: 13 g

112. TURKEY FLORENTINE

Preparation Time: 15 minutes
Cooking Time: 18 minutes
Servings: 4

Ingredients:
- 2 tablespoons olive oil
- 2 medium zucchinis (seeded, thinly sliced)
- 1/2 cup green onions (sliced)
- 2 cups turkey breast (cubed)
- 1/2 teaspoon salt
- 1/2 teaspoon thyme (ground)
- 2 tablespoons pimento (chopped)
- 3 cups cooked long-grain rice
- 4 cups fresh baby spinach
- 1/4 cup low-fat parmesan cheese (freshly grated)

Directions:
1. In a non-stick pan, heat olive oil over moderate heat. Add zucchini, turkey, and onions, stir every now and then for 5 to 10 minutes.
2. Add salt, thyme, pimento, rice, and spinach. Cook and stir for another 6-8 minutes or until heated through and spinach wilts.
3. Remove from heat, transfer to a large serving bowl, and stir in cheese. Serve.

Nutrition:
- Calories: 593
- Fat: 8 g

- Carbs: 11 g
- Fiber: 4 g
- Protein: 12 g

113. CHICKEN LETTUCE WRAPS

Preparation Time: 15 minutes
Cooking Time: 0 minutes
Servings: 2
Ingredients:
- 1/4 cup mayonnaise (low-fat)
- 2 teaspoons lemon juice
- 1/2 cup white beans (canned, cooked, drained)
- 1/3 cup feta cheese (crumbled)
- 2 tablespoons pimentos (chopped)
- 8 large lettuce leaves (washed and dried)
- 1/2 lb. cooked chicken breast strips (preferably grilled)

Directions:
1. In a medium bowl, combine mayonnaise and lemon juice.
2. Stir in beans, mashing slightly with a fork.
3. Add cheese and pimentos and mix lightly.
4. Spread lettuce leaves evenly with bean mixture.
5. Top with chicken and roll up. Serve.

Nutrition:
- Calories: 338
- Fat: 10 g
- Carbs: 39 g
- Fiber: 9 g
- Protein: 26 g

114. COUSCOUS WITH TURKEY

Preparation Time: 20 minutes
Cooking Time: 26 minutes
Servings: 4
Ingredients:
- 4 tablespoons extra-virgin olive oil
- 1 lb. turkey thighs (boneless, skinless, chopped)
- 1 onion (chopped)
- 3 garlic cloves (minced)
- 1 cup carrots (shredded)
- 1 teaspoon smoked paprika
- 1/8 teaspoon ground cinnamon
- 1/2 teaspoon salt
- 1 cup dried fruits (chopped, pitted dates, apricots)
- 4 cups turkey stock (divided)
- 2 tablespoons butter
- 1 1/2 cup couscous
- 1/2 cup Italian parsley (chopped)

Directions:
1. Set your oil to get hot on medium heat. Cook turkey and brown for 3 to 4 minutes on each side.
2. Add onions, garlic, carrots, and season with spices and salt. Cook 6-8 minutes.
3. Stir the fruits into the turkey and vegetables, and 2 ½ cups of stock.
4. Allow boiling. Turn down the heat to low, cover, and let it simmer for 10 minutes.
5. In a separate small saucepan, over medium heat, pour 1 ½ cups of stock and bring it up to a boil, then stir in the couscous.
6. Take the content off the heat and let it stand 5 minutes while the cover is on. Fluff with a fork and serve with turkey.

Nutrition:
- Calories: 469
- Fat: 24 g
- Carbs: 40 g
- Fiber: 4 g
- Protein: 18 g

115. EASY TURKEY CHILI

Preparation Time: 25 minutes
Cooking Time: 47 minutes
Servings: 4-6
Ingredients:
- 3 tablespoons olive oil
- 4 garlic cloves (minced)
- 1 medium onion (chopped)
- 1 lb. ground turkey
- 1 bay leaf
- 1 teaspoon ground cumin
- 1 teaspoon dried oregano
- 1 tomato (seeded and chopped)
- 1 (14 oz.) can tomato sauce

- 1 cup pork broth
- 1 teaspoon salt
- 2 (14 oz.) cans of red beans (drained and rinsed)

Directions:
1. Heat the oil over medium heat in a large pot and cook the onions and garlic for 5 minutes.
2. Turn the heat from medium to high. Add oregano, bay leaf, turkey, and cumin. Cook for 5-7 minutes or until the turkey has browned.
3. Add broth, tomato sauce, tomato, and salt. Once the pot is boiling, lower the heat to simmer. Let it simmer for about 20 minutes, covered.
4. If needed, add more water and beans and continue to simmer for 15 more minutes. Serve.

Nutrition:
- Calories: 193
- Fat: 13 g
- Carbs: 5 g
- Fiber: 1 g
- Protein: 16 g

116. HAM, BEAN AND CABBAGE STEW

Preparation Time: 15 minutes
Cooking Time: 17 minutes
Servings: 4

Ingredients:
- 1 tablespoon extra-virgin olive oil
- 8 oz. smoked ham (chopped)
- 1 large onion (chopped)
- 2 stalks celery (sliced)
- 5 garlic cloves (chopped finely)
- 4 cups chicken broth
- 1 (28-ounce) can tomatoes (seedless, drained)
- 3 cups whole wheat pasta
- 8 oz. coleslaw
- 2 (14-ounce) cans of kidney beans
- 1 teaspoon dried basil
- 1 teaspoon dried rosemary

Directions:
1. In a good size pot, heat olive oil over medium heat. Cook ham, onion, celery, and garlic stirring occasionally, until vegetables are tender.
2. Stir in broth and tomatoes, breaking up tomatoes. Stir the pasta in heat to boiling, and turn down the heat low.
3. Cover and simmer for about 10 minutes or until pasta is tender. Stir in coleslaw, beans, basil, and oregano.
4. Bring stew to a boil and reduce heat to low. Simmer uncovered about 5-7 minutes or until cabbage is tender.

Nutrition:
- Calories: 543
- Fat: 21 g
- Carbs: 47 g
- Fiber: 8 g
- Protein: 40 g

117. GRILLED FISH TACOS
by Ruby Edmond – Hardy

Preparation Time: 25 minutes
Cooking Time: 6 minutes
Servings: 4

Ingredients:
- 1/4 teaspoon salt
- Juice of 1/2 lemon
- 2 tablespoons olive oil
- 4 trout fillets (rinsed and dried)
- 1/2 cup red onion (chopped)
- 1/2 cup jicama (peeled, chopped)
- 1/3 cup red bell pepper (chopped)
- 2/3 cup fresh cilantro (finely chopped)
- 1/2 lime zest and juice
- 1 tablespoon plain yogurt (non-fat)
- 8 whole-wheat tortillas (warmed)

Directions:
1. Combine your oil, lemon juice, and salt.
2. Pour mixture over fish fillets and let marinate for 10 minutes. Put the fish on the grill over high heat.
3. Cook the fish on both sides for 3 minutes. In another bowl, combine onion, bell pepper, jicama, cilantro, yogurt and zest, and juice of a lime to make a salsa.
4. Add your fish on top of a warm tortilla. Top with salsa and fold in half before serving.

Nutrition:
- Calories: 356
- Fat: 9 g
- Carbs: 57 g
- Fiber: 17 g
- Protein: 15 g

118. PASTA WITH TURKEY AND OLIVES
by Stella Hickman – Baker City

Preparation Time: 20 minutes
Cooking Time: 30 minutes
Servings: 4

Ingredients:
- 1 lb. whole wheat pasta (uncooked)
- 2 teaspoons olive oil
- 1 large onion (peeled, chopped finely)
- 4 garlic cloves (peeled, finely chopped)
- 1 lb. turkey breast (cut into chunks)
- 1 teaspoon basil (dried)
- 1 teaspoon rosemary (dried)
- 12 medium black olives (pitted)
- 1 medium green bell pepper (seeded and chopped)
- 1 (14-ounce) can tomatoes (seedless, chopped)
- 1 can chicken broth
- 1/2 cup Romano cheese (shredded)

Directions:
1. Bring salted water to boil in a large pot. Add pasta and cook until al dente following the instructions according to the package.
2. While pasta cooks, heat the oil in a large pan over medium heat. Add the garlic and onion. Cook for 6 minutes.
3. Add the turkey, rosemary, and basil. Cook for about 8 minutes.
4. Stir in the olives, tomatoes, and green pepper and cook for 2 minutes. In the pan, add the chicken broth, heat the pan to a boil.
5. Reduce half of the liquid by boiling for 7 minutes. When pasta is done, add to sauce mixture.
6. Toss until pasta is evenly mixed with sauce. Top with cheese and serve.

Nutrition:
- Calories: 165
- Fat: 4 g
- Carbs: 18 g
- Fiber: 3 g
- Protein: 14 g

119. RICE BOWL WITH SHRIMP AND PEAS
by Rupert Roberts – Gulf Breeze

Preparation Time: 15 minutes
Cooking Time: 48 minutes
Servings: 4

Ingredients:
- 1 cup long-grain brown rice
- 1/4 cup soy sauce
- 1/4 cup fresh lemon juice
- 2 tablespoons rice vinegar
- 2 tablespoons honey
- 1 tablespoon olive oil
- 1 lb. shrimp (medium, cleaned, peeled, deveined)
- 8 oz. snow peas (thawed if frozen, cut in halves)
- 1 (1-inch long) shredded piece of fresh ginger
- 1 Hass avocado (chopped)

Directions:
1. Boil 2 cups of water in a saucepan. Add the rice and cover, and turn the heat down to simmer.
2. Cook the rice for about 35-45 minutes. In a bowl, fully combine soy sauce, lemon juice, honey, and vinegar.
3. Set your olive oil to get hot on medium heat in a non-stick pan.
4. Add in your shrimp, ginger, and peas, then cook for about 3 minutes (or until shrimp becomes pink).
5. Transfer rice to serving bowls, then top with avocado and shrimp mixture. Serve the sauce on the side.

Nutrition:
- Calories: 143
- Fat: 4 g
- Carbs: 19 g
- Fiber: 2 g
- Protein: 7 g

Snacks

120. RICOTTA & CANNELLINI SALAD

Preparation Time: 15 minutes
Cooking Time: 0 minutes
Servings: 6
Ingredients:
- 2 tablespoons plain yogurt (low-fat)
- 3 tablespoons extra virgin olive oil
- 2 tablespoons fresh lemon juice
- 3/4 teaspoon oregano (ground)
- 1 tablespoon fresh mint (shredded)
- 2 (14-ounce) cans of white cannellini beans (drained and rinsed)
- 1/2 cup red onions (thinly sliced)
- 3 medium tomatoes (seeded and chopped)
- 1/4 cup Greek olives (pitted)
- 1/2 cup ricotta cheese (crumbled)
- 2 cups spinach leaves

Directions:
1. In a large bowl, combine yogurt, olive oil, lemon juice, oregano, and mint; whisk well.
2. Add onion, beans, tomato, ricotta cheese, and olives; toss lightly.
3. Refrigerate for at least one hour. Serve on a bed of spinach.

Nutrition:
- Calories: 160
- Fat: 11 g
- Carbs: 10 g
- Fiber: 2 g
- Protein: 6 g

121. BEAN AND TOMATO SALAD

Preparation Time: 10 minutes
Cooking Time: 0 minutes
Servings: 4
Ingredients:
- 4 medium tomatoes (seeded and chopped)
- 2 (14-ounce) cans garbanzos (drained and rinsed)
- 1/4 cup red onions (chopped finely)
- 1 cup Italian parsley (chopped finely)
- 2 tablespoons lemon juice
- 1/4 cup extra virgin olive oil
- 1/2 teaspoon salt

Directions:
1. Combine your parsley, onions, beans, and tomato. Set aside. In another bowl, whisk together salt, olive oil, and lemon juice.
2. Pour dressing over vegetables. Mix and serve.

Nutrition:
- Calories: 201
- Fat: 14 g
- Carbs: 18 g
- Fiber: 4 g
- Protein: 4 g

122. STRING BEAN POTATO SALAD

Preparation Time: 15 minutes
Cooking Time: 7 minutes
Servings: 4-6
Ingredients:
- 1 1/2 lbs. string beans (slender)
- 6 small red potatoes (unpeeled, cubed)
- 1 small red onion (thinly sliced lengthwise)
- 1/3 cup extra virgin olive oil
- 1/4 cup red wine vinegar
- 1/4 cup rice vinegar
- 1 tablespoon garlic salt
- 1 teaspoon sugar

Directions:
1. In a pot of boiling water, cook potatoes and string beans for about 7 minutes.
2. Drain the contents and run cold water on the beans only to stop the cooking process. Drain and set it aside.
3. In a large salad bowl, combine beans, potatoes, and onions. For the dressing, in a bowl, whisk together olive oil, vinegar, garlic salt, and sugar.
4. Toss the vegetables and dressing together until coated. Refrigerate one hour prior to serving.

Nutrition:
- Calories: 142
- Fat: 11 g
- Carbs: 10 g

- Fiber: 1 g
- Protein: 1 g

123. CUCUMBER PEACH SALAD

Preparation Time: 30 minutes
Cooking Time: 0 minutes
Servings: 4
Ingredients:
- 2 large avocados (pitted and diced)
- 1 peach (unpeeled, pitted, and diced)
- 1 gala pear (unpeeled, cored, and diced)
- 1 cup cantaloupe (chopped)
- 1 shallot (chopped finely)
- 1 English cucumber (chopped)
- 1/4 cup fresh lime juice
- 1/4 cup fresh mint (chopped)
- 8 large lettuce leaves

Directions:
1. In a medium bowl, combine all ingredients except the lettuce leaves. Sprinkle the mint and lime juice.
2. Toss until combined. Let the salad sit for at least 10-20 minutes. Serve over 2 leaves of lettuce per serving.

Nutrition:
- Calories: 182
- Fat: 11 g
- Carbs: 23 g
- Fiber: 3 g
- Protein: 6 g

124. STRAWBERRY & APPLE SALAD

Preparation Time: 10 minutes
Cooking Time: 0 minutes
Servings: 2
Ingredients:
1½ cup ripe strawberries
1½ cup Fresh apple (cut in small cubes)
12 Brazil nuts (blanched and thinly sliced)
4 tablespoonfuls lemon juice
7 large lettuce leaves
1 tablespoonful dressing

Directions:
1. Cut the apples and strawberries and add Brazil nuts that have been marinated in lemon juice.
2. Shape your lettuce into a rose, and fill the lettuce with the mixture above, and cover with a spoonful salad dressing.

Nutrition:
- Calories: 184
- Fat: 11 g
- Carbs: 23 g
- Fiber: 4 g
- Protein: 4 g

125. BEAN AND COUSCOUS SALAD

Preparation Time: 15 minutes
Cooking Time: 0 minutes
Servings: 4
Ingredients:
- 1 cup couscous
- 1 1/2 cup boiling water
- 1 cup sweet yellow peppers (seeded and chopped)
- 2 cups black beans (cooked)
- 1 small onion (chopped)
- 2 cups tomatoes (seeded and chopped)
- 2 medium garlic cloves (minced)
- 1/2 cup rice vinegar
- 1/4 cup olive oil
- 1/2 teaspoon salt

Directions:
1. In a large bowl, place the couscous with boiling water. Cover and wait until the couscous has absorbed all the water.
2. Place couscous in a bowl and add the remaining ingredients. Mix well. Serve.

Nutrition:
- Calories: 637
- Fat: 15 g
- Carbs: 101 g
- Fiber: 18 g
- Protein: 28 g

126. ASIAN CHICKEN SALAD

Preparation Time: 15 minutes
Cooking Time: 0 minutes

Servings: 1

Ingredients:
- 1 cup romaine lettuce (chopped)
- 1 carrot (shredded)
- 1 celery (sliced thinly)
- 1/4 cup red pepper (seeded, sliced thinly)
- 1/2 cup chicken breast (cooked, cut into strips)
- 1/4 cup mangos (chopped)
- 2 tablespoons lime and ginger dressing

Directions:
1. Toss together all ingredients in a medium bowl until combined. Serve alone or with whole wheat bread slices.

Nutrition:
- Calories: 384
- Fat: 4 g
- Carbs: 68 g
- Fiber: 10 g
- Protein: 25 g

127. ALMOND SALAD
by Carrie W. Parker – Berlin

Preparation Time: 10 minutes
Cooking Time: 0 minutes
Servings: 1

Ingredients:
- 1½ cup blanched almonds (chopped)
- 18 olives
- 1½ cup celery (cut fine)
- 1 tablespoon salad dressing
- 5 medium lettuce leaves

Directions:
1. Stone and chop the olives. Add the almonds and the celery. Mix with salad dressing and serve on the lettuce.

Nutrition:
- Calories: 101
- Fat: 6 g
- Carbs: 10 g
- Fiber: 3 g
- Protein: 2 g

128. VEGETARIAN NUTTOLENE SALAD
by Cynthia Mora Savannah

Preparation Time: 10 minutes
Cooking Time: 0 minutes
Servings: 1

Ingredients:
- ¼ lb. nuttolene (chopped)
- 2/3 cup celery (chopped)
- ½ lb. protose (chopped)
- 1 small teaspoonful onion (grated)
- 2 lemons juice
- Salt
- 2 tablespoonfuls mayonnaise

Directions:
1. Mix all the ingredients together, then add the mayonnaise dressing last. Serve

Nutrition:
- Calories: 55
- Fat: 0 g
- Carbs: 12 g
- Fiber: 3 g
- Protein: 2 g

129. NUTTY GREEN SALAD
by Charlotte Davidson Encinitas

Preparation Time: 5 minutes
Cooking Time: 0 minutes
Servings: 4

Ingredients:
- 1 cup walnut meat
- 1 can French peas
- 1 tablespoon mayonnaise
- 1 medium lettuce

Directions:
2. Put the walnut meats in extremely hot water for fifteen minutes.
3. Remove the skins, then cut them into pieces. Set your peas to scald, then set aside.
4. Drain the water from the peas and let it get cold; then mix with the walnuts.
5. Add the mayonnaise dressing and mix thoroughly. Serve on lettuce.

- Calories: 252
- Fat: 2 g
- Carbs: 11 g
- Fiber: 4 g
- Protein: 10 g

Dinner

130. ONE-POT DINNER SOUP

Preparation Time: 15 minutes
Cooking Time: 50 minutes
Servings: 4

Ingredients:
- 1 tablespoon olive oil
- 1 cup yellow onion, chopped
- ½ cup carrots, peeled and chopped
- ½ cup celery, chopped
- 2 garlic cloves, minced
- 4 cup homemade vegetable broth
- 2½ cups sweet potatoes, peeled and chopped
- 1 cup red lentils, rinsed
- 1½ tablespoon fresh lemon juice
- Salt and freshly ground black pepper to taste
- 2 tablespoons fresh cilantro, chopped

Directions:
1. In a large Dutch oven, heat the oil over medium heat and sauté the onion, carrot, and celery for about 5-7 minutes.
2. Add the garlic and sauté for about 1 minute.
3. Add the sweet potatoes and cook for about 1-2 minutes.
4. Add in the broth and bring to a boil.
5. Reduce the heat to low and simmer, covered for about 5 minutes.
6. Stir in the red lentils and gain bring to a boil over medium-high heat.
7. Reduce the heat to low and simmer, covered for about 25-30 minutes or until desired doneness.
8. Stir in the lemon juice, salt, and black pepper and remove from the heat.
9. Serve hot with the garnishing of cilantro.

Nutrition:
- Calories: 471
- Carbs: 61 g
- Protein: 19,3 g
- Fat: 5.6 g
- Sugar: 4.4 g
- Sodium: 836 mg

- Fiber: 19.7 g

131. 3-BEANS SOUP

Preparation Time: 15 minutes
Cooking Time: 45 minutes
Servings: 12

Ingredients:
- ¼ cup olive oil
- 1 large onion, chopped
- 1 large sweet potato, peeled and cubed
- 3 carrots, peeled and chopped
- 3 celery stalks, chopped
- 3 garlic cloves, minced
- 2 teaspoons dried thyme, crushed
- 1 tablespoon red chili powder
- 1 tablespoon ground cumin
- 4 large tomatoes, peeled, seeded, and chopped finely
- 2 (16-oz.) cans great Northern beans, rinsed and drained
- 2 (15¼-oz.) cans red kidney beans, rinsed and drained
- 1 (15-oz.) can black beans, drained and rinsed
- 12 cup homemade vegetable broth
- 1 cup fresh cilantro, chopped
- Salt and freshly ground black pepper to taste

Directions:
1. In a Dutch oven, heat the oil over medium heat and sauté the onion, sweet potato, carrot and celery for about 6-8 minutes.
2. Add the garlic, thyme, chili powder, and cumin and sauté for about 1 minute.
3. Add in the tomatoes and cook for about 2-3 minutes.
4. Add the beans and broth and bring to a boil over medium-high heat.
5. Cover the pan with the lid and cook for about 25-30 minutes.
6. Stir in the cilantro and remove from heat.
7. Serve hot.

Nutrition:
- Calories: 411
- Carbs: 69.7 g
- Protein: 22.7 g
- Fat: 5.7 g
- Sugar: 7.1 g
- Sodium: 931 mg
- Fiber: 18.9 g

132. HEAVENLY TASTY STEW

Preparation Time: 15 minutes
Cooking Time: 35 minutes
Servings: 6

Ingredients:
- ¼ cup olive oil
- 1 large yellow onion, chopped
- 8 oz. fresh shiitake mushrooms, sliced
- 2 large tomatoes, chopped
- 2 tablespoons garlic, chopped finely
- 2 bay leaves
- 2 tablespoons mixed Italian herbs (rosemary, thyme, basil), chopped
- 1 teaspoon cayenne pepper
- 4 cup homemade vegetable broth
- 2 tablespoons apple cider vinegar
- 1 cup whole-wheat fusilli pasta
- 1/3 cup nutritional yeast
- 8 oz. fresh collard greens
- 1 (15-oz.) can cannellini beans, drained and rinsed
- Salt and freshly ground black pepper to taste

Directions:
1. In a large pan, heat the oil over medium heat and sauté the onion, mushrooms, potato, and tomato for about 4-5 minutes.
2. Add the garlic, bay leaves, herbs, and cayenne pepper and sauté for about 1 minute.
3. Add the broth and bring to a boil.
4. Stir in the vinegar, pasta, and nutritional yeast and again bring to a boil.
5. Reduce the heat to medium-low and simmer, covered for about 20 minutes.
6. Uncover and stir in the greens and beans.
7. Simmer for about 4-5 minutes.
8. Stir in the salt and black pepper and remove from the heat.
9. Serve hot.

Nutrition:

- Calories: 314
- Carbs: 46 g
- Protein: 14.4 g
- Fat: 10 g
- Sugar: 6.2 g
- Sodium: 489 mg
- Fiber: 12.3 g

133. THANKSGIVING DINNER CHILI

Preparation Time: 15 minutes
Cooking Time: 45 minutes
Servings: 6
Ingredients:

- 2 tablespoons olive oil
- 1 red bell pepper, seeded and chopped
- 1 onion, chopped
- 2 garlic cloves, chopped
- 1 lb. lean ground turkey
- 2 cups water
- 3 cups tomatoes, chopped finely
- 1 teaspoon ground cumin
- ½ teaspoon ground cinnamon
- 1 (15-oz.) can red kidney beans, rinsed and drained
- 1 (15-oz.) cans black beans, rinsed and drained
- ¼ cup scallion greens, chopped

Directions:

1. In a large Dutch oven, heat the olive oil over medium-low heat and sauté bell pepper, onion, and garlic for about 5 minutes.
2. Add the turkey and cook for about 5-6 minutes, breaking up the chunks with a wooden spoon.
3. Add the water, tomatoes, and spices and bring to a boil over high heat.
4. Reduce the heat to medium-low and stir in beans and corn.
5. Simmer, covered for about 30 minutes, stirring occasionally.
6. Serve hot with the topping of scallion greens.

Nutrition:

- Calories: 366
- Carbs: 40.6 g
- Protein: 28.7 g
- Fat: 11.2 g
- Sugar: 4.5 g
- Sodium: 100 mg
- Fiber: 13.4 g

134. MEATLESS MONDAY CHILI

Preparation Time: 15 minutes
Cooking Time: 1 hour 25 minutes
Servings: 4
Ingredients:

- 2 tablespoons avocado oil
- 1 medium onion, chopped
- 1 carrot, peeled and chopped
- 1 small bell pepper, seeded and chopped
- 1 lb. fresh mushrooms, sliced
- 2 garlic cloves, minced
- 2 teaspoons dried oregano
- 1 tablespoon red chili powder
- 1 tablespoon ground cumin
- Salt and freshly ground black pepper to taste
- 8 oz. canned red kidney beans, rinsed and drained
- 8 oz. canned white kidney beans, rinsed and drained
- 2 cup tomatoes, peeled, seeded and chopped finely
- 1½ cup homemade vegetable broth

Directions:

1. In a large Dutch oven, heat the oil over medium-low heat and cook the onions, carrot, and bell pepper for about 10 minutes, stirring frequently.
2. Increase the heat to medium-high.
3. Stir in the mushrooms and garlic and cook for about 5-6 minutes, stirring frequently.
4. Add the oregano, spices, salt, and black pepper and cook for about chili 1-2 minutes.
5. Stir in the beans, tomatoes, and broth and bring to a boil.
6. Reduce the heat to low and simmer, covered for about 1 hour, stirring occasionally.
7. Serve hot.

Nutrition:

- Calories: 346
- Carbs: 59.9 g
- Protein: 23.4 g
- Fat: 3.7 g
- Sugar: 10.5 g

- Sodium: 545 mg
- Fiber: 16.7 g

135. BEANS TRIO CHILI

Preparation Time: 15 minutes
Cooking Time: 1 hour
Servings: 6
Ingredients:

- 2 tablespoons olive oil
- 1 green bell pepper, seeded and chopped
- 2 celery stalks, chopped
- 1 scallion, chopped
- 3 garlic cloves, minced
- 1 teaspoon dried oregano, crushed
- 1 tablespoon red chili powder
- 2 teaspoons ground cumin
- 1 teaspoon red pepper flakes, crushed
- 1 teaspoon ground turmeric
- 1 teaspoon onion powder
- 1 teaspoon garlic powder
- Salt and freshly ground black pepper to taste
- 4½ cup tomatoes, peeled, seeded, and chopped finely
- 4 cups water
- 1 (16-oz.) can red kidney beans, rinsed and drained
- 1 (16-oz.) can cannellini beans, rinsed and drained
- ½ of (16-oz.) can black beans, rinsed and drained

Directions:

1. In a large pan, heat the oil over medium heat and cook the bell peppers, celery, scallion, and garlic for about 8-10 minutes, stirring frequently.
2. Add the oregano, spices, salt, black pepper, tomatoes, and water and bring to a boil.
3. Simmer for about 20 minutes.
4. Stir in the beans and simmer for about 30 minutes.
5. Serve hot.

Nutrition:

- Calories: 342
- Carbs: 56 g
- Protein: 20.3 g
- Fat: 6.1 g
- Sugar: 6 g

- Sodium: 79 mg
- Fiber: 21.3 g

136. STAPLE VEGAN CURRY

Preparation Time: 15 minutes
Cooking Time: 40 minutes
Servings: 6
Ingredients:

- 10 oz. whole-wheat pasta
- 1 tablespoon vegetable oil
- 1 medium white onion, chopped
- 3 garlic cloves, minced
- 1 teaspoon dried basil, crushed
- 1 tablespoon curry powder
- ¼ teaspoon red pepper flakes, crushed
- 2 lbs. ripe tomatoes, peeled, seeded, and chopped
- 4 cups cauliflower, cut into bite-sized pieces
- 1 medium red bell pepper, seeded and sliced thinly
- 1 cup water
- 1 (15-oz.) can chickpeas, drained and rinsed
- 1 cup fresh baby spinach
- ¼ cup fresh parsley, chopped
- Salt to taste

Directions:

1. In a pan of the salted boiling water, add the pasta and cook for about 8-10 minutes or according to the package's directions.
2. Drain the pasta well and set it aside.
3. Heat the oil in a large cast-iron skillet over medium heat and sauté the onion for about 4-5 minutes.
4. Add the garlic, basil, curry powder, and red pepper flakes and sauté for about 1 minute.
5. Stir in the tomatoes, cauliflower, bell pepper, and water, and bring to a gentle boil.
6. Reduce the heat to medium-low and simmer, covered for about 15-20 minutes.
7. Stir in the chickpeas and cook for about 5 minutes.
8. Add the spinach and cook for about 3-4 minutes.
9. Stir in the pasta and remove from the heat.
10. Serve hot.

Nutrition:

- Calories: 338
- Carbs: 58.4 g

- Protein: 15.1 g
- Fat: 5.9 g
- Sugar: 10.9 g
- Sodium: 80 mg
- Fiber: 10.3 g

137. FRAGRANT VEGETARIAN CURRY

Preparation Time: 15 minutes
Cooking Time: 1½ hour
Servings: 8

Ingredients:
- 8 cups water
- ½ teaspoon ground turmeric
- 1 cup brown lentils
- 1 cup red lentils
- 1 tablespoon olive oil
- 1 large white onion, chopped
- 3 garlic cloves, minced
- 2 large tomatoes, peeled, seeded and chopped
- 1½ tablespoon curry powder
- ¼ teaspoon ground cloves
- 2 teaspoons ground cumin
- 3 carrots, peeled and chopped
- 3 cup pumpkin, peeled, seeded, and cubed into 1-inch size
- 1 granny smith apple, cored and chopped
- 2 cup fresh spinach, chopped
- Salt and freshly ground black pepper to taste

Directions:
1. In a large pan, add the water, turmeric, and lentils over high heat and bring to a boil.
2. Reduce the heat to medium-low and simmer, covered for about 30 minutes.
3. Drain the lentils, reserving 2½ cups of the cooking liquid.
4. Meanwhile, in another large pan, heat the oil over medium heat and sauté the onion for about 2-3 minutes.
5. Add in the garlic and sauté for about 1 minute.
6. Add the tomatoes and cook for about 5 minutes.
7. Stir in the curry powder and spices and cook for about 1 minute.
8. Add the carrots, potatoes, pumpkin, cooked lentils, and reserved cooking liquid and bring to a gentle boil.
9. Reduce the heat to medium-low and simmer, covered for about 40-45 minutes or until the desired doneness of the vegetables.
10. Stir in the apple and spinach and simmer for about 15 minutes.
11. Stir in the salt and black pepper and remove from the heat.
12. Serve hot.

Nutrition:
- Calories: 263
- Carbs: 47 g
- Protein: 14.7 g
- Fat: 2.9 g
- Sugar: 9.7 g
- Sodium: 53 mg
- Fiber: 20 g

138. OMEGA-3 RICH DINNER MEAL
by Shirley Mills – Cherry Hill

Preparation Time: 15 minutes
Cooking Time: 40 minutes
Servings: 4

Ingredients:
For Lentils:
- ½ lb. French green lentils
- 2 tablespoons extra-virgin olive oil
- 2 cup yellow onions, chopped
- 2 cup scallions, chopped
- 1 teaspoon fresh parsley, chopped
- Salt and freshly ground black pepper to taste
- 1 tablespoon garlic, minced
- 1½ cup carrots, peeled and chopped
- 1½ cup celery stalks, chopped
- 1 large tomato, peeled, seeded, and crushed finely
- 1½ cup chicken bone broth
- 2 tablespoons balsamic vinegar

For Salmon:
- 2 (8-oz.) skinless salmon fillets
- 2 tablespoons extra-virgin olive oil
- Salt and freshly ground black pepper to taste

Directions:
1. In a heat-proof bowl, soak the lentils in boiling water for 15 minutes.

2. Drain the lentils completely.

3. In a Dutch oven, heat the oil over medium heat and cook the onions, scallions, parsley, salt, and black pepper for about 10 minutes, stirring frequently.

4. Add the garlic and cook for about 2 more minutes.

5. Add the drained lentils, carrots, celery, crushed tomato, and broth and bring to a boil.

6. Reduce the heat to low and simmer, covered for about 20-25 minutes.

7. Stir in the vinegar, salt, and black pepper and remove from the heat.

8. Meanwhile, for salmon: preheat your oven to 450°F.

9. Rub the salmon fillets with oil and then season with salt and black pepper generously.

10. Heat an oven-proof sauté pan over medium heat and cook the salmon fillets for about 2 minutes without stirring.

11. Flip the fillets and immediately transfer the pan into the oven.

12. Bake for about 5-7 minutes or until the desired doneness of salmon.

13. Remove from the oven and place the salmon fillets onto a cutting board.

14. Cut each fillet into 2 portions.

15. Divide the lentil mixture onto serving plates and top each with 1 salmon fillet.

16. Serve hot.

Nutrition:
- Calories: 707
- Carbs: 50.2 g
- Protein: 16.1 g
- Fat: 29.8 g
- Sugar: 7.9 g
- Sodium: 496 mg
- Fiber: 16.2 g

139. WEEKEND DINNER CASSEROLE
by Marjorie E. Peer – Bakersfield

Preparation Time: 20 minutes
Cooking Time: 1 hour
Servings: 6

Ingredients:
- 2½ cups water, divided
- 1 cup red lentils
- ½ cup wild rice
- 1 teaspoon olive oil
- 1 small onion, chopped
- 3 garlic cloves, minced
- 1/3 cup zucchini, peeled, seeded and chopped
- 1/3 cup carrot, peeled and chopped
- 1/3 cup celery stalk, chopped
- 1 large tomato, peeled, seeded, and chopped
- 8 oz. tomato sauce
- 1 teaspoon ground cumin
- 1 teaspoon dried oregano, crushed
- 1 teaspoon dried basil, crushed
- Salt and freshly ground black pepper to taste

Directions:

1. In a pan, add 1 cup of the water and rice over medium-high heat and bring to a rolling boil.

2. Reduce the heat to low and simmer, covered for about 20 minutes.

3. Meanwhile, in another pan, add the remaining water and lentils over medium heat and bring to a rolling boil.

4. Reduce the heat to low and simmer, covered for about 15 minutes.

5. Transfer the cooked rice and lentils into a casserole dish and set aside.

6. Preheat your oven to 350°F.

7. Heat the oil in a large skillet over medium heat and sauté the onion and garlic for about 4-5 minutes.

8. Add the zucchini, carrot, celery, tomato, and tomato paste and cook for about 4-5 minutes.

9. Stir in the cumin, herbs, salt, and black pepper and remove from the heat.

10. Transfer the vegetable mixture into the casserole dish with rice and lentils and stir to combine.

11. Bake for about 30 minutes.

12. Remove from the heat and set aside for about 5 minutes.

13. Cut into equal-sized 6 pieces and serve.

Nutrition:
- Calories: 192
- Carbs: 34.5 g
- Protein: 11.3 g
- Fat: 1.5 g
- Sugar: 3.9 g
- Sodium: 239 mg
- Fiber: 12 g

140. FAMILY DINNER PILAF
by Linda Levesque – Grass Valley

Preparation Time: 15 minutes
Cooking Time: 1 hour
Servings: 4

Ingredients:
- 2 tablespoons olive oil
- 2 garlic cloves, minced
- 2 cups fresh mushrooms, sliced
- 1¼ cup brown rice, rinsed
- 2 cups homemade vegetable broth
- Salt and freshly ground black pepper, to taste
- 1 red bell pepper, seeded and chopped
- 4 scallions, chopped
- 1 (16-oz.) can red kidney beans, drained and rinsed
- 2 tablespoons fresh parsley, chopped

Directions:
1. In a large pan, heat the oil over medium heat and sauté the onion for about 4-5 minutes.
2. Add the garlic and mushrooms and cook for about 5-6 minutes.
3. Stir in the rice and cook for about 1-2 minutes, stirring continuously.
4. Stir in the broth, salt, and black pepper and bring to a boil.
5. Reduce the heat to low and simmer, covered for about 35 minutes, stirring occasionally.
6. Add in the bell pepper and beans and cook for about 5-10 minutes or until all the liquid is absorbed.
7. Serve hot with the garnishing of parsley.

Nutrition:
- Calories: 463
- Carbs: 76.7 g
- Protein: 18.5 g
- Fat: 10.1 g
- Sugar: 3.2 g
- Sodium: 431 mg
- Fiber: 11.6 g

Dessert

141. WHOLE-WHEAT-CHOCOLATE CHIP COOKIES

Preparation Time: 10 minutes
Cooking Time: 10 minutes
Servings: 48

Ingredients:
- 1 cup (225 g) unsalted butter
- 1/4 cup (64 g) peanut butter
- 1 cup (340 g) honey
- 2 eggs
- 1 ½ cup whole-wheat pastry flour
- 1 teaspoon baking soda
- 2 cups (160 g) rolled oats
- 2 cups (350 g) chocolate chips
- 1 cup (110 g) chopped pecans

Directions:
1. Cream together the first 4 ingredients.
2. Add the next 5 ingredients and mix well.
3. Add enough flour for a stiff dough.
4. Drop by teaspoons on a baking sheet.
5. Bake at 375°F (190°C, gas mark 5) for 10 minutes.

Nutrition:
- Calories: 365
- Fat: 7 g
- Sodium: 629 mg
- Carbs: 67 g
- Sugar: 16 g
- Protein: 14 g
- Saturated Fat: 1 g
- Fiber: 18 g
- Cholesterol: 0 g

142. GOOD-FOR-YOU CHOCOLATE CHIP COOKIES

Preparation Time: 10 minutes
Cooking Time: 10 minutes
Servings: 36
Ingredients:

- 1/4 cup (55 g) unsalted butter
- 1 cup (150 g) packed brown sugar
- 1/4 cup (85 g) honey
- 1 egg
- 1 teaspoon vanilla extract
- 1/4 cup (60 ml) skim milk
- 1 teaspoon baking soda
- 1/2 teaspoon baking powder
- 1 cup (82 g) granola
- 3/4 cup quick-cooking oats
- 2 cups whole-wheat pastry flour
- 1 cup (175 g) chocolate chips

Directions:
1. Cream the butter and brown sugar.
2. Mix in honey, egg, vanilla, and milk, then baking soda and baking powder.
3. Add granola, oats, and flour. Mix all ingredients.
4. Stir in chocolate chips.
5. Place on a non-stick baking sheet in teaspoons.
6. Bake at 325°F (170°C, gas mark 3) for 10 minutes.

Nutrition:
- Calories: 287
- Fat: 19 g
- Saturated Fat: 3 g
- Fiber: 6 g
- Cholesterol: 0 g
- Carbs: 18 g
- Sodium: 451 g
- Sugar: 6 g

143. OAT AND WHEAT COOKIES

Preparation Time: 10 minutes
Cooking Time: 12-15 minutes
Servings: 4
Ingredients:
- 3/4 cup (165 g) unsalted butter
- 1/2 cup (130 g) peanut butter
- 1 cup (150 g) brown sugar
- 1 ¼ cup (150 g) whole-wheat pastry flour
- 1 teaspoon baking soda
- 1 ¼ cup (100 g) rolled oats

Directions:
1. Mix all ingredients.
2. Set by rounded teaspoons onto an ungreased baking sheet.
3. Bake at 375°F (190°C, gas mark 5) for 10-12 minutes or until golden brown.
4. Let rest on the baking sheet for 1 minute and then cool on racks.

Nutrition:
- Calories: 124
- Cholesterol: 0 g
- Saturated Fat: 0 g
- Fiber: 3 g
- Carbs: 22 g
- Sugar: 5 g
- Protein: 2 g
- Fat: 3 g

144. OATMEAL SPICE COOKIES

Preparation Time: 10 minutes
Cooking Time: 30 minutes
Servings: 48
Ingredients:
- 1 cup (145 g) raisins
- 1 cup (235 ml) water
- 1/2 cup (112 g) unsalted butter, softened
- 1/4 cup (60 ml) vegetable oil
- 1 ½ cup (300 g) sugar
- 2 eggs
- 1 teaspoon vanilla extract
- 2 ½ cups (300 g) whole-wheat pastry flour
- 1/2 teaspoon baking powder
- 1 teaspoon baking soda
- 2 teaspoons cinnamon
- 1/4 teaspoon nutmeg
- 2 cups (160 g) quick-cooking oats
- 1/2 cup (60 g) chopped walnuts

Directions:
1. Preheat the oven to 350°F (180°C, gas mark 4).
2. Simmer the raisins and water in a saucepan on low until plump, for approximately 20 minutes.
3. Drain the liquid into the measuring cup and add water to make 1/2 cup of liquid.
4. Cream butter, oil, and sugar.

5. Add eggs and vanilla.
6. Stir in the raisin liquid.
7. Sift the flour and spices; add to the sugar mixture.
8. Add oats, nuts, and raisins.
9. Set by rounded teaspoons onto an ungreased baking sheet.
10. Flatten slightly and then bake 8-10 minutes or until slightly brown.

Nutrition:
- Calories: 357
- Sodium: 768 mg
- Cholesterol: 8 g
- Carbs: 54 g
- Sugar: 5 g
- Protein: 14 g

145. TRAIL MIX COOKIES

Preparation Time: 10 minutes
Cooking Time: 10 minutes
Servings: 60
Ingredients:
- 3/4 cup (165 g) unsalted butter
- 3/4 cup (150 g) sugar
- 1 egg
- 1 teaspoon vanilla extract
- 2 cups whole-wheat pastry flour
- 1 teaspoon baking soda
- 1 teaspoon cinnamon
- 1/4 teaspoon nutmeg
- 3/4 cup (175 ml) skim milk
- 1 ¾ cup (140 g) quick-cooking oats
- 1 ½ cup (200 g) trail mix

Directions:
1. Cream the butter and sugar. Add egg and vanilla; beat well. Stir the dry ingredients.
2. Attach them to the mixture alternately with milk, mixing well.
3. Stir in oats and the trail mix. Set by tablespoons on a baking sheet covered with non-stick vegetable oil spray.
4. Bake at 400°F (200°C, gas mark 6) until lightly browned, 8-10 minutes.

Nutrition:
- Calories: 413
- Fat: 20 g
- Carbs: 7 g
- Sugar: 1 g
- Fiber: 1 g
- Protein: 50 g
- Sodium: 358 mg

146. WHITE CHOCOLATE-CRANBERRY COOKIES

Preparation Time: 10 minutes
Cooking Time: 10 minutes
Servings: 36
Ingredients:
- 1/2 cup (112 g) shortening
- 1 cup (225 g) brown sugar
- 1 egg
- 1 teaspoon vanilla extract
- 13/4 cups (210 g) whole-wheat pastry flour
- 1 teaspoon baking soda
- 1/4 cup (60 ml) buttermilk
- 1/2 cup (87 g) white chocolate chips
- 1/2 cup (60 g) dried cranberries

Directions:
1. Beat the shortening until light. Add sugar and beat until fluffy.
2. Beat in the egg and vanilla.
3. Stir the dry ingredients. Attach them to mixture alternately with buttermilk.
4. Beat until smooth. Stir in chips and cranberries.
5. Drop about 2 inches (5 cm) apart on a baking sheet coated with non-stick vegetable oil spray.
6. Bake at 375°F (190°C, gas mark 5) for 8-10 minutes, until lightly browned.

Nutrition:
- Calories: 361
- Fat: 10 g
- Saturated Fat: 2 g
- Cholesterol: 0 g
- Sodium: 139 mg
- Fiber: 14 g

147. OATMEAL SUNFLOWER BREAD
by Katherine Castillo – Pleasantville

Preparation Time: 10 minutes
Cooking Time: 20 minutes
Servings: 12

Ingredients:
- 1 cup (235 ml) water
- 1/4 cup (85 g) honey
- 2 tablespoons (28 g) unsalted butter
- 3 cups (411 g) bread flour
- 1/2 cup (40 g) quick-cooking oats
- 2 tablespoons non-fat dry milk powder
- 2 teaspoons yeast
- 1 tablespoon vital wheat gluten
- 1/2 cup (72 g) unsalted shelled sunflower seeds

Directions:
1. Set all ingredients except the sunflower seeds in a bread machine in order specified by the manufacturer.
2. Process on a large white loaf cycle.
3. Add the sunflower seeds at the beep or 5 minutes before the end of kneading.

Nutrition:
- Calories: 599
- Fat: 19 g
- Carbs: 9 g
- Sugar: 4 g
- Fiber: 2 g
- Protein: 97 g
- Sodium: 520 mg

148. MAPLE OATMEAL BREAD
by Ann D. Lee – Gatlinburg

Preparation Time: 10 minutes
Cooking Time: 20 minutes
Servings: 12

Ingredients:
- 1 ¾ teaspoon yeast
- 1 cup (157 ml) warm water
- 2 ½ cups (342 g) bread flour
- 1/2 cup flour
- 1 cup (27 g) rolled oats
- 1 cup (80 ml) maple syrup
- 1/4 cup (17 g) non-fat dry milk
- 2 tablespoons (28 g) unsalted butter, room temperature

Directions:
1. Add all ingredients to the bread machine in the order specified by the manufacturer.
2. Process on a sweet bread or whole-wheat cycle.

Nutrition:
- Calories: 238
- Carbs: 27 g
- Sugar: 12 g
- Saturated Fat: 2 g
- Fiber: 6 g
- Cholesterol: 39 g
- Protein: 21 g

149. GERMAN DARK BREAD
by Hollie J. Wilborn – Kingstree

Preparation Time: 10 minutes
Cooking Time: 20 minutes
Servings: 12

Ingredients:
- 1 cup (235 ml) water
- 1/4 cup (85 g) molasses
- 1 tablespoon unsalted butter
- 2 cups (274 g) bread flour
- 1 ¼ cup (160 g) rye flour
- 2 tablespoons cocoa powder
- 1 ½ teaspoon yeast
- 1 tablespoon vital wheat gluten

Directions:
1. Set all ingredients in the bread machine in order specified by the manufacturer. Process on a whole-wheat cycle.

Nutrition:
- Calories: 287
- Fat: 19 g
- Saturated Fat: 3 g
- Fiber: 6 g
- Cholesterol: 0 g
- Carbs: 18 g
- Sodium: 451 mg

150. ONION AND GARLIC WHEAT BREAD
by Justine Otey – Chicago

Preparation Time: 10 minutes
Cooking Time: 20 minutes
Servings: 12

Ingredients:
- 1/2 cup (80 g) finely chopped onion
- 1/2 teaspoon finely chopped garlic
- 1 tablespoon sugar
- 1/2 cup whole-wheat flour
- 2 ½ cups (342 g) bread flour
- 1 ½ tablespoon non-fat dry milk
- 1 ½ teaspoon yeast
- 3/4 cup (175 ml) water
- 1 ½ tablespoon (21 g) unsalted butter

Directions:
1. Set all ingredients in the bread machine in order specified by the manufacturer. Process on a white bread cycle.

Nutrition:
Calories: 329
Fat: 17 g
Carbs: 9 g
Sugar: 3 g
Fiber: 5 g
Protein: 37 g

CHAPTER 7
MENTAL APPROACH TO THE DISORDER, DEVELOPING RESILIENCE

Being able to adjust to life's issues and setbacks is referred to as resilience. Test your level of resiliency and get advice on how to improve it.

When you have resilience, you can draw on inner strength to help you recover from a setback or struggle, especially if it is related to an illness. You may linger on difficulties, feel victimized, become overwhelmed, or resort to unhealthy coping techniques, such as substance misuse if you lack resilience.

Resilience won't make your issues go away, but it can help you see past them, find joy in life, and deal with stress more effectively. If you aren't as resilient as you'd like to be, you can improve your resilience by learning new abilities.

ADAPTING TO ADVERSITY IS A SKILL THAT MAY BE LEARNED

The ability to adapt to adversity is referred to as resilience. You still feel wrath, grief, and anguish when stress, hardship, or trauma occurs, but you're able to operate—both physically and psychologically. Resilience, on the other hand, isn't about enduring adversity, being stoic, or sorting things out on your own. In fact, one of the most important aspects of resilience is the ability to seek help from others.

MENTAL HEALTH AND RESILIENCE

Resilience can aid in the prevention of mental illnesses, such as sadness and anxiety. The struggles caused by the illness might increase the likelihood of mental health problems. Resilience can help offset these risks and can help you cope better.

TIPS FOR BOOSTING YOUR RESILIENCY

Consider the following suggestions if you want to become more resilient:

Establish a connection. In both good and terrible times, having strong, positive relationships with loved ones and friends may give you much-needed support and acceptance. Volunteering or joining a church or spiritual community can help you make other crucial relationships.

Make each and every day count. Every day, do something that makes you feel accomplished and with purpose. Make a list of goals to help you look forward to the future with purpose.

Learn from your mistakes. Consider how you've dealt with adversity in the past. Consider the abilities and methods that aided you in overcoming adversity. You may also keep a journal of your past experiences to help you identify positive and negative behavior patterns, as well as to guide your future conduct.

Don't lose hope. You can't undo what is happening, but you can always look forward. Accepting and even anticipating change makes it easier to adjust and cope with new problems.

Look after yourself. Pay attention to your own wants and emotions. Participate in hobbies and activities that you enjoy, also considering your current physical status. Make sure you get enough rest. Maintain a balanced diet. Yoga, meditation, guided visualization, deep breathing, and prayer are examples of stress management and relaxation strategies.

Take the initiative. Don't put off dealing with your issues. Instead, determine what needs to be done, devise a strategy, then do it. Although it may take time to recover, keep in mind that if you work hard enough, your condition will improve.

CHAPTER 8
EMOTIONAL RESILIENCE AND MEDITATION EXERCISES

The key to developing emotional resilience and well-being is to concentrate on the things you can control.

Barriers between family, career and self have been blurred for parents. Making time for mental wellness is extremely crucial for them. "Self-care is not an afterthought, but something planned out, even if it's only for two or five minutes a day," she continues. It's critical to show your children how to do this."

PACED BREATHING CAN HELP YOU DEAL WITH ANXIETY

"Take a minute every day to concentrate on your breathing." Here's how to do it:

Inhale deeply through your nose and exhale deeply through your mouth.

Slowly and deeply inhale until your lungs are fully inflated.

Exhale slowly until your lungs are completely empty.

"Deep breathing offers short-term and long-term benefits in reducing stress and anxiety."

AVOID FALLING INTO "THINKING TRAPS"

In times of uncertainty, it's crucial to reflect on our own thoughts. Learning the talent will benefit you for the rest of your life.

Thinking in black-and-white terms: assuming that everything is either perfect or amazing or that everything is horrible.

Catastrophic thinking is when you expect the worst possible event and believe you won't be able to cope if it happens.

Predicting the future: Assuming you know what will happen in the future (for example, "I won't be able to go back to school, I'll never receive the degree I require, and I won't attend college").

How to stay out of these snares:

Catch yourself: Recognize when you're about to fall into a trap. You may begin to feel depressed, anxious, or hopeless.

Think more realistically or holistically: Ask yourself, or discuss with a trusted friend or family member, what is real and what isn't real about your views. Where are the ambiguous areas? Are you overlooking more feasible "in-between" possibilities?

Create a coping mantra: Think of a phrase that will help you respond to your problems. "I'm doing the best I can, and I'll be fine," you could say.

"Being able to control the intensity of our emotions can lead to more self-care and more effective behavior for our mental health."

MAINTAIN A GRATITUDE NOTEBOOK

A thankfulness habit can help even little children. Make a list of three things you loved and were grateful for during the day in a notepad or journal. It could be something as simple as a tasty snack, quality time with a pet, or something you witnessed outside.

"Think of a silver lining for the day," says the narrator. "How we feel can be affected by that adjustment in thinking. It can assist us in managing our emotions and the actions we take in response."

PARTICIPATE IN BEHAVIORAL ACTIVATION EXERCISES

"Being behaviorally stimulated gives our moods a boost." Physical activity, such as exercise, can be considered behavioral activation. However, any activity that gives you a sensation of control and action might be included. You could try the following activation methods:

Physical activation includes things like exercise, dancing, deep breathing, and relaxing your muscles. Try these five bone-strengthening exercises for people who have Gaucher disease.

Thoughts and feelings: Activation can be achieved through creative undertakings such as painting, drawing, or even jigsaw puzzles. Outward-focused activities, such as a service project that benefits others, can also be beneficial.

Mastery: Developing a new skill might provide you with a sense of accomplishment. You may utilize this time to practice your instrument or study a language with an app.

Sensory: You may make a self-soothing kit to assist you to calm down and ground yourself when you're feeling anxious. Include something to appeal to each of your five senses: something aesthetically appealing, a pleasant odor, and tactile, auditory, and gustatory experiences.

"When we're upset or experiencing strong emotions, we typically feel compelled to withdraw. The desire to avoid things is a common symptom of anxiety. However, from a behavioral standpoint, it may be beneficial to consider the opposite action—interacting with others and being interested." "We may take little measures to confront fear in a safe manner."

For example, coronavirus may make you nervous about going to a doctor's appointment. Make an informed decision by assessing the risks and advantages. Wear a mask, wash your hands, and maintain social space to help you center yourself and realize you're fine.

KEEP TRACK OF HOW MUCH TIME YOU SPEND ON

YOUR DEVICE AND HOW MUCH NEWS YOU CONSUME

It might be difficult to stay informed in today's always-on society without becoming overwhelmed. Adults, teens, and children are all affected by the availability of smartphones, tablets, and a continual stream of information.

Prior to COVID, studies revealed that excessive usage of electronics could raise anxiety and depression in youth who are predisposed to feeling anxious and depressed. During the pandemic, however, social media served as a method for teens and tweens to stay in touch.

"The trick is to strike a healthy balance between socializing with friends and getting work done. It shouldn't be about the number of likes on an Instagram photo or the fear of losing out." "For parents, that means keeping the lines of communication open about what makes sense for their family and what's best for them."

Adults find it difficult to spend so much time in front of a screen. Zoom fatigue and screen weariness are both real. It's a terrific time to get creative with doing things outside as a family now that school is out and the weather is getting nicer. During this time, we all need technology to stay connected.

But, whether it's writing letters or going for bike rides, balance your device time with old-school means of having fun and pleasure.

"It's fine to interact with pals through social media or gaming, and it's also fine to set a limit."

GUIDED MEDITATION 1

As you sit comfortably and breathe at this moment, take a second to bring your awareness to your root chakra. With this newfound, newly placed awareness, imagine a red light surrounding you and let yourself feel safe, secure, and protected. As you can, keep this light going throughout the entire meditation for your root chakra.

Now, as we begin this meditation, try to draw your breath all the way down into the very base of your root chakra. Since your awareness is already down there, it should be a little easier to feel like your breath can make its way there, too. With a calm and steady breath, now try to imagine that you can grow roots from this root chakra, just like a tree does. As you sit comfortably and breathe at this moment, imagine that you are a tree.

GUIDED MEDITATION 2

Locate a calm spot where there will be no interferences. Turn off all your diverse electronic gadgets, so they don't occupy you while ruminating. You will need to absolutely unwind, and you won't have the capacity to do that with your telephone beside you. You can incorporate distinctive smoothing components around you, for example, plants, or blossoms, or possibly you need to light a flame. At whatever point, you are prepared to begin your reflection, locate an agreeable stance and close your eyes.

Imagine a modest wad of red light at the region. This light is exceptionally powerless and needs recuperating. Take a full breath in through your nose and aid the air towards your root territory. Envision the air as a wind loaded with vitality and affection. At the point when the air achieves the root chakra, perceive how the territory starts to shine, and the red light gets brighter and bigger. Presently breathe out the air and envision yourself breathing out negative energies from your chakra. The now brighter red wad of light at the root takes in the vitality from the air and turns into a touch littler once more, yet more extraordinary.

Take another full breath, like some time recently. Pretty much as you did sometime recently, envision that the air you are currently breathing out is depleted air that expels all antagonism from your chakra. Envision the red wad of light getting more grounded, brighter, and all the more effective for every inward breath that you take. Take as much time as required and don't surge this activity. Attempt to truly feel the distinction.

As the vitality ball keeps on getting bigger and bigger, it will start to extend from your body and achieve your air. The light will break out into you're encompassing emanation and invigorate that too.

GUIDED MEDITATION 3

Find a comfortable position, either laying down or sitting, and take in three deep and slow breaths. With each inhale, imagine the breath sending energy to your perineum; this is the space between your anus and genitals. With every exhale, release whatever you are holding in this area. This could be pain or fear. It could even be what you think you should be feeling while in this meditation.

Begin to gently tap at the top of your pubic bone or on either side of the lower parts of your hips. This will wake up the connection you have with your root chakra.

As you continue to breathe in and out through your nose, direct your breath to your chakra. Picture a red glowing light growing and pulsing in your lower pubic area. For people who identify mostly as male, the light should spin clockwise. For people who identify mostly as female, the light should spin counterclockwise.

Take some more breaths to notice if you get any feedback. This feedback could be a word, intuition, color, image, song, sound, or feeling. Act upon the feedback you receive. If nothing comes up, you don't need to worry about it. You will get something as you continue to practice.

If you didn't receive a message, but you start to feel a new awareness in your root chakra, something like a pulsating in the lower hips and down through your feet, you have made a connection to your root chakra.

As your meditation comes to a close, take three deep and slow breaths. Direct your inhales towards your feet so that you are grounded, and then slowly open your eyes.

Make sure you take things slowly as you start. This will take some time and practice, so be patient. If you end up feeling any sort of pain in your legs or lower back, you are trying too hard. Take a break and go back to it later. Remember that even seasoned meditators will sometimes find it hard to shut off their mind. Take this moment to observe these thoughts without judging them; let them go and gently refocus your mind.

GUIDED MEDITATION 4

Let's establish a mantra for now. How about this one: "I am strong and sturdy, like an age-old tree. I make roots in the land and have roots in the earth through my core and my very own base. Like the tree, I grow and make seeds. Like the tree, my roots are vast and endless. I am an eternity of calm. I am what grows." Repeat the mantra again with me: "I am strong and sturdy, like an age-old tree. I make roots in the land and have roots in the earth through my core and my very own base. Like the tree, I grow and make seeds. Like the tree, my roots are vast and endless. I am an eternity of calm. I am what grows." If this mantra is too long for you, choose one sentence from what I've just said – the one sentence that stuck out the most—and repeat that one phrase instead.

As you repeat this mantra, again and again, remember what you visualized before with the tree and its roots and its branches and remember how this all relates to your own body and your own future experience. With each repetition, be like a tree: firm, secure, confident, strong, tall, and inspired. Feel connected with your root to the earth. Feel open with possibility as the mantra becomes condensed into one pure, vibrational, energetic expression of hope.

GUIDED MEDITATION 5

Find a comfortable position, either laying down or sitting. Take in three deep and slow breaths. With each inhale, imagine the breath sending energy to the space right below your belly button. With every exhale, release whatever you are holding in this area. This could be pain or fear. It could even be what you think you should be feeling while in this meditation. You can place your hand on this area while you meditate if you would like.

Begin to gently tap the area below your belly button with two fingers. You can also gently massage the area in a circular motion.

As you continue to breathe in and out through your nose, direct your breath to your chakra. Picture an orange glowing light growing and pulsing in your lower abdomen area. For people who identify mostly as male, the light should spin clockwise. For people who identify mostly as female, the light should spin counterclockwise.

Take some more breaths to notice if you get any feedback. This feedback could be a word, intuition, color, image, song, sound, or feeling. Act upon the feedback you receive. If nothing comes up, you don't need to worry about it. You will get something as you continue to practice.

If you didn't receive a message, but you start to feel a new awareness in your sacral chakra, something like a pulsating in this area, you have made a connection to your sacral chakra.

As your meditation comes to a close, take three deep and slow breaths. Direct your inhales towards your feet so that you are grounded, and then slowly open your eyes.

Make sure you take things slowly as you start. This will take some time and practice, so be patient. If you end up feeling any sort of pain in your lower abdomen, you are trying too hard. Take a break and go back to it later.

GUIDED MEDITATION 6

Find a comfortable position; in this guided meditation, you have a choice of either sitting up with your legs crossed or laying down on a bed or couch. To make sure that you won't fall asleep during the meditation, take away your pillow from underneath your head or add an extra one; it will help your body notice that this is not your usual sleeping position, thus making it easier to stay awake. If you have chosen to sit up, make sure to straighten your spine as you breathe in to ensure the flow of energy through your spine and other chakras. Place your palms on your knees and form a 'mudra' hand position. If you have chosen to lay down, then proceed by straightening your body and laying down facing upwards.

Start off by bringing your awareness to the way your body moves as you inhale or exhale in the chest area. Gradually allow your eyes to close slowly and but not forcefully. Make sure that you are maintaining a well-balanced breathing pattern that is smooth, deep, and slow. By focusing and keeping your watch over the way you breathe, you are allowing for the mind and body to relax.

Once your body is fully relaxed, bring your attention to your stomach and organs and expand as you breathe in and out. Breathe deeply and watch your stomach rise instead of your lungs; this helps to cleanse the lower abdomen area and activate the sacral chakra. Continue to breathe deeply, relaxing your body in the process and observing your lower abdomen. Return to your awareness of the way you breathe in, as your organs are expanding and changing their shape when you inhale or exhale through your stomach.

Whether you are laying down or sitting up, raise your hands and place them on the lower abdomen, skin to skin. Visualize a warming light radiating from the lower abdomen, picture an orange glow lighting up, and warm up your hands as well as the sacral region. Bring forth your intention to open and balance the sacral chakra. You will begin to feel some tingling and movements in your lower abdomen, but don't let it distract your concentration.

Visualize the light evolving and glowing brighter than before, with the feeling of warmth and tingling sensations slowly spreading all throughout the body. Stay in this moment and enjoy the butterflies and the joyous feelings in your stomach. Each time you deeply inhale, bring that orange glow a tiny bit brighter and bigger.

If you have a specific spot within the body or the sacral region that you want to heal, then direct that energy there with the intention to receive healing. Allow yourself to sit in that feeling for a couple of minutes, reminding yourself of your pure intentions, before gently opening your eyes. Breathe in the air around you and look around as you still feel that strong and bright energy. The energy will overwhelm you with a strong urge to create, so allow it to guide you in releasing the energy and inspiration.

GUIDED MEDITATION 7

Begin by sitting in an easy pose position; close your eyes breathing deeply and regularly. When meditating for the sacral chakra, tuck your chin down a little bit to help open up the spine to increase energy flow. If you feel comfortable doing this and have the privacy to do so, it can really heighten the experience.

Start by imagining a glowing white disk in front of you. Hold your breath for three to five seconds as you breathe. Start to see the disk rotating, slowly at first. As it rotates, see the disk gradually assume an orange color. Visualize the orange color gradually filling up the disk as it spins faster with time, generating more energy. Now, feel the ball of light enter your body, rising slowly and assuming a deeper and brighter orange color as it moves up to your root chakra. Keep visualizing it, and imagine the glowing disk fully assuming a deep, bright, and energetic orange color.

Be consciously aware of all the sensations, and in particular, feel sensations of heat as they arise. You can also visualize warming, glowing orange energy covering the area of the chest. Do not be shy; enjoy healthy sexuality to the fullest while maintaining natural control. The mediations will help you to arrive at this place in your life.

Now, imagine the orange disk rising into your brain. This will help elevate your creativity and have healthy fantasies that are not destructive and don't become obsessions. You can end the meditation at this point.

GUIDED MEDITATION 8

Start your meditation by getting comfortable; sit down with your legs crossed, your spine straight and reach out as high as possible.

Make sure your head is not sulking, but nice straight and tall.

Your head should face the front as the chin is raised, imagine as if you are balancing a book on your head.

Form a mudra with your hands, an 'okay' or 'zero' look-a-like sign by uniting the thumb and the index finger together before placing it on top of your knees, the palm of your hand facing upwards.

Begin by taking a few minutes to relax your body and muscles, focus your attention on your breathing as your chest rises and falls.

Breathe in deeply, inhale through your nose and hold your breath for up to three seconds before exhaling it through the mouth and dragging it out for another three seconds.

Make sure that when you are breathing in and out that you expand your chest instead of breathing through your stomach.

Feel the way your lungs expand inside of you as they are filled with the air around you, cleansing you, and getting both your mind and body ready for the pure energy of your life force energy.

The purpose of this meditation is to take your worries away from your inability to speak up, so try not to let the feelings of worry and anxiety take over. This is your time to let go of all the bad thoughts and let you be the person you are meant to be as well as heal the throat and shoulder region.

Take a few minutes to simply relax your muscles and the body as you breathe in.

Bring your attention to your breathing as you inhale and exhale to help calm the mind.

Imagine yourself to be one with the universe as the energy flows through your body.

Relax the different parts of your body, including your throat and neck.

As you breathe in, feel how the air comes through your nostrils, to your throat, and into your lungs before coming back up.

It is clearing all the negative energy out when you inhale and lets it all go as you exhale.

Breath in deeply, form a rhythm of your body.

Begin the usual energy harnessing by calling out to the Universe and making an intention to harness your life force energy.

Imagine a white light emitting from within your body, spreading all throughout.

Allow for your mind's goals to be clear by setting an intention to receive healing within the throat area and helping yourself speak up more and become more involved with the community through the healing found within the chakra.

Focus on centering your energy within your hands. Imagine the white light surrounding you, traveling all the way to your hands.

Let the energy catch up and gather there, forming a bright ball of light.

Lift your hands up and place them on your collar bone, one hand over the other.

Visualize the healing energy leaving your hands and sinking deep through your body and making its way to the center of the throat chakra.

While allowing the pure white energy to settle down, begin to visualize the color blue, think of the first emotion or thing that pops into your head.

Feel your body calming down and becoming more stable.

Then picture that color blue evolving through your throat, a gently blue glow expanding every time you inhale, merging together with the energy of the white.

But just thinking about it can bring forth feelings of worry, so imagine all that worry resurfacing and letting it go as you breathe out.

This is your voice and your own opinions; you have the right to express what is really in your heart.

This is also a perfect time to release any stress or worries that you might have by simply bringing them back up to the surface and making an intention for the bright blue light to simply purify them.

Let go of anything that might be bothering you.

Feel the tingling and warmth sensations through your neck as they emerge and push you to want to open your mouth and speak whatever is on your mind.

Bring an intention forward to receive physical healing through the healing of the mind.

Visualize that glow becoming bigger and brighter for three to five minutes before drawing your attention back to your breathing.

While still holding your hands on that area, use the mantra 'ham' which can create vibrations that have the power to alter the flow of energy within the communication center.

Once you spend at least two to three minutes healing that part of your body, move your hands upward and extend the healing energy to your throat.

Hold your hands there for another brief two to three minutes before rotating and moving them to the back of your neck.

Allow for the white energy to sink in right around the throat while releasing the blue energy of the throat chakra, bringing in healing and relaxation to that area.

Visualize the tensions going away, the muscles relaxing.

Hold your hands against your throat for a minute before moving down towards your shoulders.

Allow for the blue light to intervene with the white, creating a light blue hue.

Let that healing energy work its magic, traveling and releasing any negative tensions within the shoulder area.

Rest that energy against the shoulders for a brief minute.

Allow for the energy to evenly spread throughout your body, returning back to its original state, this time more powerful.

Imagine the body relaxing and energizing itself as your life force energy returns back throughout your body, purifying along the way.

Continue to deeply breathe in and out for about a minute, simply resting in the newfound sensation.

Slowly bring your attention to your body, the way you breathe, or the weight that your body holds against the earth below you.

Open your eyes. Remain seated in complete silence for another minute, allowing for the healing energy to further settle in while you take some time to reflect on your meditation.

To finish off the treatment, tell someone what is on your mind or sing your favorite songs before carrying on with your day.

GUIDED MEDITATION 9

Get a comfortable chair in a room and sit down. Ensure this room is free from any distractions for the duration of time you are meditating.

Practice inhaling and exhaling ten times, as deep as you can. Remember to inhale through your nose but breathe out through your mouth.

From the top of your head, scan your body carefully while listening to the air going in and out of your body. Feel your muscles relax as you scan each part of your body.

Once the scan is complete, visualize a spinning ball of blue light floating at your throat level. This bulb of light is growing and keeps getting brighter the more you focus on it.

The bulb of light grows in size and becomes brighter. At this point, all your relaxation and feelings of openness are centered towards the light.

Embrace the energy and let it travel all through your body. Once you can feel the energy all over your body, open your eyes slowly.

You can take a few minutes to embrace the moment before your meditation session is over.

GUIDED MEDITATION 10

Find a quiet, safe, and secluded space.

Begin by sitting in a cross-legged pose with your back and spine straight and your shoulders relaxed but held firmly back.

Move to a position in which you are kneeling, with your upper body bent forward and supported by your hands on the ground, facing forward, parallel with your knees. Your back will resemble a table, with your upper legs and arms acting as the four table legs.

As you inhale deeply, lift your tail upward, drop your belly toward the floor, and stretch your neck as your head looks upward.

As you exhale, tuck your tail under, arch your back upward, and you're your head and neck downward as you gaze toward your belly button.

Maintain each position from 30 to 60 seconds.

If you feel comfortable, after a few repetitions, you may open your throat further by exhaling forcefully through your mouth while chanting the Sanskrit syllable, "ham."

GUIDED MEDITATION 11

Sit on in the easy pose position. You might want to slightly tilt your head back during this meditation to open up the throat area. The addition of a blue cushion helps to bring more blue light energy to the meditation while also helping to elevate the spine a little bit, helping to open the throat chakra.

Close your eyes and begin breathing calmly. See a blue ball of light against the inky blackness of space, and imagine it slowly approaching you. As the ball of light moves through space, see the shades of blue change, starting from a light shade of baby blue, progressing through turquoise colors, and gradually darkening into the rich blue colors of lapis lazuli stones. Then, see it gradually lighten and have it repeat the color sequence.

See this ball of light come closer and closer until it is right in front of you, bathing your body in soft blue light. Begin inhaling deeply, and see the light energy enter your lungs, passing through the throat area and healing the larynx. Then see the blue light energy filling your entire body and then exhale, and see the blue light gradually leave the body.

Keep repeating this exercise for 15-30 minutes, with the color of the light changing gradually so that you can inhale the light of different energy levels. This will help you to heal all aspects of the throat chakra, from having insecurity about speaking your own truth to being able to listen to others and heal them.

GUIDED MEDITATION 12

This meditation is best practiced in a seated position, but you may also practice it lying down.

Begin by breathing deeply, filling your lungs, and moving your breath down into the center of your neck. With each exhale, release your breath down through your shoulders, arms, and out through your palms and fingertips.

Visualize a cerulean blue wheel of light originating in the center of your throat. Watch the circle of light opens outward as it spins, whirling slowly at first and then a bit faster. With each exhale, feel this whirling blue healing light open up even more and move out into your aura and energetic field. Keep going until it's about six feet wide. Think of this whirling portal as a megaphone. If you could whisper into it, the energy would powerfully project into the universe.

Consider chanting your mantra to help open up this piece of your visualization. Once your energetic throat center is open, call to mind three scenarios in which you currently feel things are out of balance. Pay attention to your daily habits and life circumstances by taking a brief inventory. Are you projecting more yang (masculine) energy or yin (feminine) energy into the situation?

Perhaps there is a certain area where you need to step in, speak up, and take charge. Invite in yang energy to help here. Or maybe you need to loosen the reins a bit and let go of your need to control; in this case, invite in more yin energy because yang energy is overactive.

If there are more than three years of your life that feel out of balance, make a mental list. This may include your work, finances, love life, family life, spirituality, or inspiration. Call up one solution that would bring fulfillment, happiness, and equilibrium to a part of your life. Take time to connect with the purpose behind your solution. Your purpose and solution may evolve as new layers are illuminated.

As you notice yourself coming into a solution mindset or simply gaining the capacity to find spaciousness for the solution, invite positive energy into your throat space. This healing energy can bring nourishment. With your exhale, release all that no longer serves you.

Before you seal your practice, chant, tone, or hum into your blue chakra wheel. Bring the energy of the chakra wheel down and gradually shrink it into the throat space center. Notice the light growing smaller until the wheel has stopped swirling and your throat space is glowing with cerulean blue light at the center.

Consider making an agreement with yourself to continue caring for your mind and body beyond your sit. Finally, honor yourself for bringing your throat space back into alignment.

GUIDED MEDITATION 13

Settle yourself into a comfortable seated position, either on the ground or in a chair, with your feet firmly on the ground. Maintain proper posture with your spine straight but not rigid. Place your hands in your lap with your palms up; this will aid in your willingness to receive. Gently close your eyes and take a few deep breaths in through your nose and out through your mouth. Scan your body for any areas of tension, paying particular attention to any feelings of tension or constriction in your chest. Breathe into those areas until you begin to feel them release.

Visualize a 12-petaled green lotus flower in your heart chakra, its petals tightly closed. As you breathe into your heart chakra, each inhale begins to make the lotus glow. With each exhale, its petals begin to open.

As you chant, an emerald green light begins to expand from the lotus flower. With each exhale, the love expands and spreads out of your heart chakra, filling your entire body and then the room around you. Imagine the light spreading even further now, through your town, your country, and eventually covering the entire world with the light of cosmic love.

Continue this breathing pattern and visualization until you feel the warmth of prana's love filling and emanating from your heart chakra, being received and given in equal measure. When you are ready to end your meditation, imagine the green light slowly receding back into your heart chakra, where it waits, ready to be carried again on the air of your breath. Release the visualization and take a few deep closing breaths. Wiggle your fingers and toes and stretch your neck from side to side. When you are ready, open your eyes and return to the room.

Do this meditation any time you feel the flow of love blocked in your life.

GUIDED MEDITATION 14

Lie down on a flat surface. Make sure that you are comfortable. Close your eyes.

Take a deep breath and then slowly exhale. Do this two more times.

Next, breathe in and place your arms around your body, giving yourself a hug. And as you breathe out, stretch your arms to your sides and allow them to rest on the floor.

Lying on your back, feel your vulnerability as a person but also allow yourself to feel your connection to the earth.

Lie still and take a few more deep breaths, but always exhaling slowly.

Keeping your eyes closed, visualize that you are releasing all negative energies as you exhale.

With every exhalation, allow yourself to let go of all stagnant and harmful energies such as greed, anger, hate, and jealousy.

And when you inhale, visualize the new and positive life energies flowing throughout your body.

Listen to the rhythm of your breathing. This is the beating of your heart. Every beat is significant because new energy enters your body. Every heartbeat should remind you that you are capable of giving love and receiving love.

Allow your body and mind to feel calm

This time as you breathe in, let the love that is flowing freely around you enter your heart.

As you exhale, send out the love that you have and feel for the people around you.

Allow the love to fill your body.

Continue laying down for a while. Use this time to cleanse your heart of any fear, anger, hate, envy, and resentment.

Now, when you are ready, slowly open your eyes and share the love that you feel to your family, friends, and special someone.

Spread the love that you feel in your heart to other people as well and receive any love that comes your way.

GUIDED MEDITATION 15

The key to healing the heart and chest area is through music.

Begin by picking a soft melody with gentle beats and sounds, no lyrics, so you won't be able to sing along in your head.

It is scientifically proven that the right music can make you feel happier, so make sure you find something that you feel a certain connection to.

Turn it on by a few bars that are soft enough to hear but not that loud, for example, 1/4 of the music bars.

Make sure that the melody is longer than ten minutes or on repeat.

Begin by laying down and relaxing comfortably.

Place a pillow under your head and another under your knees for utmost comfort.

Leave your hands lying next to your body with the palms facing up.

Take a minute to focus and clear your mind by breathing in deeply.

Breathe in from your nose, hold your breath for two seconds and exhale through your mouth.

Continue this easy and simple breathing technique for a minute.

Inhale through the nose, and exhale through the mouth while setting a mental intention to relax your body as much as you can.

Proceed by gently closing your eyes and giving all of your attention to your chest area.

Use your lungs when you are breathing instead of your stomach.

This means that when you breathe in, allow for your lungs to expand, moving around, filling them up with oxygen.

Make sure that all of your attention is centered on your chest and the way it rises and falls or the way your body stretches upwards as you breathe in or shrinks as you breathe out.

Imagine that with every breath you take, you clear out the negativity within the chest, releasing it through the mouth and allowing for yourself to let go of any tensions or impurities.

As you allow for your body to relax further and as you become more familiar with the deep breathing rhythm of your body, begin to listen carefully to the different tunes that you hear and try to focus on a specific one that stands out to you.

For example, if it's the sound of the bells you hear, then bring your focus there.

Try to push away any thoughts that might be emerging to the back of your head and relax while listening to that soft and quiet sound.

Take a moment to appreciate the music that you are hearing.

Observe how that melody makes you feel emotional. Are you feeling happiness and love in your heart? If so, then continue by visualizing your heart fluttering as if it is opening up to love.

Think of flower petals emerging through your heart, floating around you, ready to travel to your loved ones.

Keep in touch with your own emotion of love and connect it to the flower petals.

Think of a person close to you, a friend, a lover, or a family member. Think of sending them those pink or green glowing petals filled with your love and empathy.

Wish them happiness and abundance throughout their life.

Picture those petals flowing to wherever they are now and connecting with their hearts.

Do this with two or three other people that you hold close to your heart.

Feel the warmth and tingling as more petals leave your heart and travel to your loved ones.

Let the energy gathered within your heart be released through your body, spread love throughout it, and feel it within you.

Let the energy run freely up and down your spine through all the chakras, uniting them and growing your spiritual growth.

Proceed by making an intention to resurface the energy and asking the universe for guidance in this practice.

Focus on the white auric field surrounding your body, making you feel safe and comfortable.

You will begin to feel tingling sensations and warmth in different parts of your body.

Let the healing energy take its time resurfacing within your body and allow for it to center exactly where the heart is.

As you do the petal release exercise, your heart becomes more pure and positive, allowing energy to access it more easily.

Place an intention to receive protection from anything negative in your life, negative events, negative emotions, and negative people.

This will help you feel safer and at ease from negativity.

Place another intention of receiving self-healing energy targeting the specific part of your body, the chest.

Allow for that energy to move from the heart to the shoulders and down to the palms of your hands, all connecting with one another.

Channel your energy and concentrate on centering it on your hands.

Allow the flow of white energy to resurface in your palms and glow a white and pure color.

Take a minute to just let all of the energy catch up and gather in that area, healing the hands along the way.

Lift both of your hands and place them on your heart, one over the other.

Allow the energy to sink into your heart chakra and visualize the white-colored light changing into a bright green, which is associated with the heart chakra.

Focus on feeling the beat of your heart against your hands, feel the pulsing vibrations underneath.

Rest at the moment as that green light sinks in deeper into your chest.

Allow the energy to circulate and explore the chest area, going exactly where tensions are present.

Feel the tingling sensations throughout your body, smell the air around you as you take in deep breaths, hear the soft melody echoing in the room or against your ears, taste the freedom and the love life gives you, and finally, although your eyes are closed, notice the glowing green light emerging through your heart.

Visualize the color glowing brighter and brighter as it opens your heart chakra to all the love and happiness that you deserve.

Think of different times when love was expressed and given to you. Even the small things that made you happy still count!

Open yourself to healing within your heart.

Use the mantra 'yam' to help you open this chakra further.

Spend some time to open your chakra, don't rush through the process but let your body heal its heart, either physically or emotionally.

Finish up by deeply breathing in and out through your mouth for a few minutes, just focusing on the music and the emotional feelings you receive from it.

The point of this meditation is to make you feel love to live, love for others around you, especially for yourself, and heal your chest area with positive and pure energy.

When you think you have finished, take some time for the energy to settle within your body for a minute or two.

Allow for your eyes to slowly open, adjusting them to the light and the physical world around you.

Make sure to reflect on the meditation that you have just performed and the healing that you have received.

Proceed by doing something that makes you happy or something that you love.

Take some time to relax after the healing process, don't push yourself to do anything.

Stay at home, relax, take a hot bath, and let your body heal while the energy within your body is still present.

CHAPTER 9
HOW TO MANAGE TROUBLESOME SYMPTOMS WITH MEDITATIONS, MINDFULNESS, YOGA, EXERCISES ACCORDING TO YOUR PERSONALITY

Do you spend a lot of time and energy trying to control and stop your symptoms, or are they so ingrained in your life that it seems impossible to get through each day without them? If either is the case, you are not alone.

With the help of these simple psychological techniques, you can find peace within yourself by managing troublesome symptom that drains us mentally and physically.

A) UTILIZE MINDFULNESS TO CONTROL SYMPTOMS

Mindfulness is an ancient Buddhist meditation tool that has been used for thousands of years to achieve peace of mind and tranquility. This technique teaches one to deal with problems without reacting by keeping one's attention on the present moment. As a result, you can develop the ability to see patterns in your physical reactions and, therefore, lessen your symptoms.

With mindfulness techniques, you can control symptoms just by paying attention to them, rather than forcing yourself not to react or become angry. See below about mindfulness exercises.

B) LEARN HOW YOUR BRAIN AFFECTS SYMPTOMS BY USING MEDITATIONS/MINDFULNESS EXERCISES

The important thing to remember is the brain you have today is not the same as it was yesterday because each day, brain cells are regenerating and evolving. In contrast to what we were taught in science class, we now know that we can reshape our brains through meditation and mindfulness.

The good news is that our brains become more resilient and less reactive as we age. It has been found that practicing living mindfully and meditating every day for an hour will help you feel less stressed and more able to cope with your symptoms.

C) UTILIZE YOGA TO CONTROL SYMPTOMS

Yoga classes help release stress by focusing on breathing techniques, movement of limbs, and meditation. Practicing yoga in a class can help you to focus and master appropriate breathing techniques for many of your symptoms.

D) LEARN THE PROPER EXERCISES ACCORDING TO YOUR PERSONALITY TYPE AND HOW THEY'LL HELP YOU TO COPE WITH SYMPTOMS

As mentioned earlier, each person has a different personality type. So it is important to know which types of exercise suits you best so that you will be able to understand how the body feels and what to do with it. For example, someone with an INFJ (Introverted, Intuitive, Feeling, and Judging) personality type would benefit from:

1-EXERCISE: Find small ways to empower yourself.

Try learning karate, biking, or even hiking for this purpose.

Manage symptoms by exploring your surroundings and the world by doing the things you like.

2-EXERCISE: Use positive visualization techniques.

By imagining pleasant, joyful experiences in your mind, you can create an internal image that controls symptoms. For example, if your symptoms are due to stress and pressure, try picturing a part of nature and take deep breaths as you do this.

This will help regulate the amount of natural endorphins that we release into our bodies to alleviate symptoms.

3-EXERCISE: Find an exercise that balances you.

Due to this personality type being one of the most difficult to maintain balance, try using a bicycle or walking for an hour a day.

This will help you focus on the present moment, which helps manage symptoms.

4-EXERCISE: Have a proper diet to control symptoms.

It is important to maintain your weight by eating healthy meals, reducing your refined sugar intake, and portioning out what you eat into smaller portions instead of one big meal. Taking supplements is also suggested for this personality type to help with feelings of depression or being overwhelmed by stress.

CHOOSE THE RIGHT KIND OF COMPLEMENTARY MENTAL ACTIVITY FOR YOU

Choosing the right kind of complementary mental activity will help you manage your symptoms and achieve a healthier lifestyle. Here are some simple suggestions for those who do not know where to start:

1-EXERCISE:

Stretch and do yoga poses first thing in the morning and watch how you can conquer your day.

2-EXERCISE:

Try engaging in activities that help you feel good about yourself. For example, volunteering at a local animal shelter or picking up trash on a hike.

3-EXERCISE:

Be creative and try to unwind through painting, photography, or playing music.

These activities will help you relax and allow you to become more positive about yourself.

4-EXERCISE:

Try some slower-paced activities, like gardening, cooking, or taking piano lessons. These activities will help balance your mind and give you a sense of accomplishment that can be helpful in dealing with symptoms on an everyday basis.

5-EXERCISE:

Help yourself feel good by doing things that interest you. Try getting out of the house and buying new things for yourself, like clothes or a book. These small purchases can help lift your spirits and make you feel more positive about yourself.

6-EXERCISE:

Even simple things like having a bubble bath or reading a book can help you relax and feel good about yourself.

CHAPTER 10

ILLUSTRATION OF YOGA TECHNIQUES, MINDFULNESS, AND CONCEPTS ON HOW TO INCREASE RESILIENCE

Yoga gives people a solid balance of mindfulness and physical exercise. It's one of the most effective methods to keep your mind healthy and stress levels normal, which boosts your overall quality of life. Yoga also helps you to conquer pain, reconnect with yourself, and focus on what's important. Plus, it trains you in leadership skills so that you can share this practice with others! If you haven't started yet, I highly recommend giving this amazing practice a try. If any individual movement doesn't appeal to you right away, these yoga techniques provide many alternatives so you can master them quickly

Yoga will not only improve your health but also help give back the balance necessary to find that happiness within us all. So how can we do that?

1. RELAX INTO THE MOMENT

The first step is to relax into the moment. This means you stop rushing from one thing to another and acknowledge what's going on in front of you. Think about what's actually happening right here, right now, and what you think or feel about it. I find this very useful when I'm about to eat something unhealthy or on the verge of losing my temper! It helps me remain calm and more present in whatever situation I'm facing—and it works almost every time! A personal tool I use for this is a very short version of a meditation exercise called "mindful breathing." It involves paying attention to my breath. If I notice that my mind is wandering from a particular thought or a stressful situation, I pay attention to my breath and empty out any negative emotions, thoughts, or worries. Then I focus on the present moment. Through this exercise, you can regain your presence and focus your mind entirely on what's going on right in front of you.

2. FOCUS ON THE 'WHY' NOT JUST THE 'WHAT'

Focusing on what you want out of life is a good way to stay motivated and energized with no regrets when your future self looks back at this time in your life. One of the best ways to stay motivated is to ask yourself "why" you are doing something. It's one of the most powerful tools to help you achieve your goals. When you really know why you are doing something, it's far easier to push through any obstacles or challenges that come your way while seeing your true purpose. Giving yourself a reason for why you're moving forward with each decision will make every step count towards your greater goal!

3. FIND BALANCE IN ALL THINGS

A lot of us believe that there's only one way to live, act, and make decisions. But the truth is that there are many paths to achieve your goals in life. I'm not saying you shouldn't be yourself or stick to certain rules. What I'm trying to say is that instead of thinking there's only one right path, it's better to take many small "mini-steps" towards your goals. If you have a specific goal in mind, try spending some time exploring other things. Just being around these different experiences every day will help you grow and learn from everything you see or do, making your overall journey much more meaningful and fulfilling!

4. FIND THE MEANING BEHIND EACH DECISION

"As for me, I'll do what I want, when I want to." This quote is attributed to The Beatles, but I think it's true in all aspects of our lives. The truth is that everyone has the right to be themselves and follow their own path to success. But you have to learn how to manage yourself well in order for you not to miss an opportunity or risk making a bad decision when you should know better. You can't always take risks because you might end up getting hurt or disappointed in the end! But living your life by finding your purpose is one of the most fulfilling experiences.

CHAPTER 11
12 WEEKS MEAL PLAN

WEEK 1

Day	Breakfast	Lunch	Snacks	Dinner	Dessert
1	Strawberry Apple Juice	Homey Clear Chicken Broth	3-Ingredient Sugar-Free Gelatin	Chicken Vegetable Soup	Gala Apple Flavored Ice Cubes
2	Fall Energizer Juice	Asian Inspired Wonton Broth	Cranberry Kombucha Jell-O	Carrot Ginger Soup	Kale Flavored Ice Cubes
3	Mushroom, Cauliflower and Cabbage Broth	Oxtail Bone Broth	Strawberry Gummies	Turkey Sweet Potato Hash	Cranberry Flavored Ice Cubes
4	Ginger, Mushroom and Cauliflower Broth	Beef Bone Broth	Fruity Jell-O Stars	Chicken Tenders with Honey Mustard Sauce	Banana Ice Cubes
5	Fish Broth	Indian Inspired Vegetable stock	Plum and Nectarine Gelatin Pudding	Chicken Breasts with Cabbage and Mushrooms	Elderberry Gummies
6	Clear Pumpkin Broth	Homey Clear Chicken Broth	3-Ingredient Sugar-Free Gelatin	Duck with Bok Choy	Blackberry-Rose Ice Pops
7	Pork Stock	Asian Inspired Wonton Broth	Cranberry Kombucha Jell-O	Beef with Mushroom and Broccoli	Frozen Strawberry-Peach Pops

WEEK 2

Day	Breakfast	Lunch	Snacks	Dinner	Dessert
1	Breakfast Cereal	Garden Veggies Quiche	Almond Peanut Butter Fudge	Chicken Cutlets	Papaya-Mango Smoothie
2	Sweet Potato Hash with Sausage and Spinach	Fluffy Pumpkin Pancakes	Quick Cocoa Mousse	Slow Cooker Salsa Turkey	Cantaloupe Smoothie
3	Cajun Omelet	Super-Tasty Chicken Muffins	Cinnamon Pear Chips	Sriracha Lime Chicken and Apple Salad	Cantaloupe-Mix Smoothie
4	Strawberry Cashew Chia Pudding	Classic Zucchini Bread	Chocolate Yogurt Cream & Roasted Bananas	Pan-Seared Scallops with Lemon-Ginger Vinaigrette	Applesauce-Avocado Smoothie
5	Peanut Butter Banana Oatmeal	Greek Inspired Cucumber Salad	Coconut Celery Smoothie	Roasted Salmon and Asparagus	Pina Colada Smoothie
6	Overnight Peach Oatmeal	Light Veggie Salad	Apple Spinach Smoothie	Cod with Ginger and Black Beans	Diced Fruits
7	Mediterranean Salmon and Potato Salad	Eastern European Soup	Banana Cocoa Cream	Halibut Curry	Applesauce

WEEK 3

Day	Breakfast	Lunch	Snacks	Dinner	Dessert
1	Pear Turkey Pita	Pork and Penne Pasta	Ricotta & Cannellini Salad	One-Pot Dinner Soup	Whole-wheat–Chocolate Chip Cookies
2	Overnight Oats	Chicken and Quinoa Pita	Bean and Tomato Salad	3-Beans Soup	Good-for-You Chocolate Chip Cookies
3	Veggie Scramble	Chicken and Asparagus Pasta	String bean Potato Salad	Heavenly Tasty Stew	Oat and Wheat Cookies
4	Turkey and Avocado Pitas	Turkey Florentine	Cucumber Peach Salad	Thanksgiving Dinner Chili	Oatmeal Spice Cookies
5	Grilled Vegetable Sandwich	Chicken Lettuce Wraps	Strawberry & Apple Salad	Meatless Monday Chili	Trail Mix Cookies
6	Spinach and Ham Pizza	Couscous with Turkey	Bean and Couscous Salad	Beans Trio Chili	White Chocolate-Cranberry Cookies
7	Fruit Bowl	Pork and Penne Pasta	Asian Chicken Salad	Staple Vegan Curry	Oatmeal Sunflower Bread

WEEK 4

Day	Breakfast	Lunch	Snacks	Dinner	Dessert
1	Ginger, Mushroom and Cauliflower Broth	Homey Clear Chicken Broth	3-Ingredient Sugar-Free Gelatin	Chicken Tenders with Honey Mustard Sauce	Elderberry Gummies
2	Fish Broth	Asian Inspired Wonton Broth	Cranberry Kombucha Jell-O	Chicken Breasts with Cabbage and Mushrooms	Blackberry-Rose Ice Pops
3	Clear Pumpkin Broth	Oxtail Bone Broth	Strawberry Gummies	Duck with Bok Choy	Frozen Strawberry-Peach Pops
4	Pork Stock	Beef Bone Broth	Fruity Jell-O Stars	Beef with Mushroom and Broccoli	Honey Lemonade Popsicles
5	Slow Cooker Pork Bone Broth	Indian Inspired Vegetable stock	Plum and Nectarine Gelatin Pudding	Beef with Zucchini Noodles	Orange Strawberry Popsicles
6	Homemade No Pulp Orange Juice	Homey Clear Chicken Broth	Homemade Lemon Gelatin	Spiced Ground Beef	Melon Basil Moscow Mule Popsicles
7	Apple Orange Juice	Asian Inspired Wonton Broth	Sour Blueberry Gummies	Ground Beef with Veggies	Honeydew Mint Homemade Popsicles

WEEK 5

Day	Breakfast	Lunch	Snacks	Dinner	Dessert
1	Peanut Butter Banana Oatmeal	Classic Zucchini Bread	Chocolate Yogurt Cream & Roasted Bananas	Pan-Seared Scallops with Lemon-Ginger Vinaigrette	Applesauce-Avocado Smoothie
2	Overnight Peach Oatmeal	Greek Inspired Cucumber Salad	Coconut Celery Smoothie	Roasted Salmon and Asparagus	Pina Colada Smoothie
3	Mediterranean Salmon and Potato Salad	Light Veggie Salad	Apple Spinach Smoothie	Cod with Ginger and Black Beans	Diced Fruits
4	Pea Tuna Salad	Eastern European Soup	Banana Cocoa Cream	Halibut Curry	Applesauce
5	Carrot and Turkey Soup	Citrus Glazed Carrots	Homemade Pumpkin Pie	Chicken Cacciatore	Avocado Dip
6	Creamy Pumpkin Soup	Spring Flavored Pasta	Zero Sugar Pumpkin Pie	Chicken and Bell Pepper Sauté	Homemade Hummus
7	Chicken Pea Soup	Gluten-Free Curry	Orange Curd	Chicken Salad Sandwiches	Tofu

WEEK 6

Day	Breakfast	Lunch	Snacks	Dinner	Dessert
1	Veggie Scramble	Turkey Florentine	String bean Potato Salad	Heavenly Tasty Stew	Oatmeal Spice Cookies
2	Turkey and Avocado Pitas	Chicken Lettuce Wraps	Cucumber Peach Salad	Thanksgiving Dinner Chili	Trail Mix Cookies
3	Grilled Vegetable Sandwich	Couscous with Turkey	Strawberry & Apple Salad	Meatless Monday Chili	White Chocolate-Cranberry Cookies
4	Spinach and Ham Pizza	Easy Turkey Chili	Bean and Couscous Salad	Beans Trio Chili	Oatmeal Sunflower Bread
5	Fruit Bowl	Ham, Bean and Cabbage Stew	Asian Chicken Salad	Staple Vegan Curry	Maple Oatmeal Bread
6	Easy Tofu & Beans	Grilled Fish Tacos	Almond Salad	Fragrant Vegetarian Curry	German Dark Bread
7	Couscous with Dates	Pasta with Turkey and Olives	Vegetarian Nuttolene Salad	Omega-3 Rich Dinner Meal	Onion and Garlic Wheat Bread

WEEK 7

Day	Breakfast	Lunch	Snacks	Dinner	Dessert
1	Strawberry Apple Juice	Homey Clear Chicken Broth	3-Ingredient Sugar-Free Gelatin	Chicken Vegetable Soup	Gala Apple Flavored Ice Cubes
2	Fall Energizer Juice	Asian Inspired Wonton Broth	Cranberry Kombucha Jell-O	Carrot Ginger Soup	Kale Flavored Ice Cubes
3	Mushroom, Cauliflower and Cabbage Broth	Oxtail Bone Broth	Strawberry Gummies	Turkey Sweet Potato Hash	Cranberry Flavored Ice Cubes
4	Ginger, Mushroom and Cauliflower Broth	Beef Bone Broth	Fruity Jell-O Stars	Chicken Tenders with Honey Mustard Sauce	Banana Ice Cubes
5	Fish Broth	Indian Inspired Vegetable stock	Plum and Nectarine Gelatin Pudding	Chicken Breasts with Cabbage and Mushrooms	Elderberry Gummies
6	Clear Pumpkin Broth	Homey Clear Chicken Broth	3-Ingredient Sugar-Free Gelatin	Duck with Bok Choy	Blackberry-Rose Ice Pops
7	Pork Stock	Asian Inspired Wonton Broth	Cranberry Kombucha Jell-O	Beef with Mushroom and Broccoli	Frozen Strawberry-Peach Pops

WEEK 8

Day	Breakfast	Lunch	Snacks	Dinner	Dessert
1	Breakfast Cereal	Garden Veggies Quiche	Almond Peanut Butter Fudge	Chicken Cutlets	Papaya-Mango Smoothie
2	Sweet Potato Hash with Sausage and Spinach	Fluffy Pumpkin Pancakes	Quick Cocoa Mousse	Slow Cooker Salsa Turkey	Cantaloupe Smoothie
3	Cajun Omelet	Super-Tasty Chicken Muffins	Cinnamon Pear Chips	Sriracha Lime Chicken and Apple Salad	Cantaloupe-Mix Smoothie
4	Strawberry Cashew Chia Pudding	Classic Zucchini Bread	Chocolate Yogurt Cream & Roasted Bananas	Pan-Seared Scallops with Lemon-Ginger Vinaigrette	Applesauce-Avocado Smoothie
5	Peanut Butter Banana Oatmeal	Greek Inspired Cucumber Salad	Coconut Celery Smoothie	Roasted Salmon and Asparagus	Pina Colada Smoothie
6	Overnight Peach Oatmeal	Light Veggie Salad	Apple Spinach Smoothie	Cod with Ginger and Black Beans	Diced Fruits
7	Mediterranean Salmon and Potato Salad	Eastern European Soup	Banana Cocoa Cream	Halibut Curry	Applesauce

WEEK 9

Day	Breakfast	Lunch	Snacks	Dinner	Dessert
1	Pear Turkey Pita	Pork and Penne Pasta	Ricotta & Cannellini Salad	One-Pot Dinner Soup	Whole-wheat–Chocolate Chip Cookies
2	Overnight Oats	Chicken and Quinoa Pita	Bean and Tomato Salad	3-Beans Soup	Good-for-You Chocolate Chip Cookies
3	Veggie Scramble	Chicken and Asparagus Pasta	String bean Potato Salad	Heavenly Tasty Stew	Oat and Wheat Cookies
4	Turkey and Avocado Pitas	Turkey Florentine	Cucumber Peach Salad	Thanksgiving Dinner Chili	Oatmeal Spice Cookies
5	Grilled Vegetable Sandwich	Chicken Lettuce Wraps	Strawberry & Apple Salad	Meatless Monday Chili	Trail Mix Cookies
6	Spinach and Ham Pizza	Couscous with Turkey	Bean and Couscous Salad	Beans Trio Chili	White Chocolate-Cranberry Cookies
7	Fruit Bowl	Pork and Penne Pasta	Asian Chicken Salad	Staple Vegan Curry	Oatmeal Sunflower Bread

WEEK 10

Day	Breakfast	Lunch	Snacks	Dinner	Dessert
1	Ginger, Mushroom and Cauliflower Broth	Homey Clear Chicken Broth	3-Ingredient Sugar-Free Gelatin	Chicken Tenders with Honey Mustard Sauce	Elderberry Gummies
2	Fish Broth	Asian Inspired Wonton Broth	Cranberry Kombucha Jell-O	Chicken Breasts with Cabbage and Mushrooms	Blackberry-Rose Ice Pops
3	Clear Pumpkin Broth	Oxtail Bone Broth	Strawberry Gummies	Duck with Bok Choy	Frozen Strawberry-Peach Pops
4	Pork Stock	Beef Bone Broth	Fruity Jell-O Stars	Beef with Mushroom and Broccoli	Honey Lemonade Popsicles
5	Slow Cooker Pork Bone Broth	Indian Inspired Vegetable stock	Plum and Nectarine Gelatin Pudding	Beef with Zucchini Noodles	Orange Strawberry Popsicles
6	Homemade No Pulp Orange Juice	Homey Clear Chicken Broth	Homemade Lemon Gelatin	Spiced Ground Beef	Melon Basil Moscow Mule Popsicles
7	Apple Orange Juice	Asian Inspired Wonton Broth	Sour Blueberry Gummies	Ground Beef with Veggies	Honeydew Mint Homemade Popsicles

WEEK 11

Day	Breakfast	Lunch	Snacks	Dinner	Dessert
1	Peanut Butter Banana Oatmeal	Classic Zucchini Bread	Chocolate Yogurt Cream & Roasted Bananas	Pan-Seared Scallops with Lemon-Ginger Vinaigrette	Applesauce-Avocado Smoothie
2	Overnight Peach Oatmeal	Greek Inspired Cucumber Salad	Coconut Celery Smoothie	Roasted Salmon and Asparagus	Pina Colada Smoothie
3	Mediterranean Salmon and Potato Salad	Light Veggie Salad	Apple Spinach Smoothie	Cod with Ginger and Black Beans	Diced Fruits
4	Pea Tuna Salad	Eastern European Soup	Banana Cocoa Cream	Halibut Curry	Applesauce
5	Carrot and Turkey Soup	Citrus Glazed Carrots	Homemade Pumpkin Pie	Chicken Cacciatore	Avocado Dip
6	Creamy Pumpkin Soup	Spring Flavored Pasta	Zero Sugar Pumpkin Pie	Chicken and Bell Pepper Sauté	Homemade Hummus
7	Chicken Pea Soup	Gluten-Free Curry	Orange Curd	Chicken Salad Sandwiches	Tofu

WEEK 12

Day	Breakfast	Lunch	Snacks	Dinner	Dessert
1	Veggie Scramble	Turkey Florentine	String bean Potato Salad	Heavenly Tasty Stew	Oatmeal Spice Cookies
2	Turkey and Avocado Pitas	Chicken Lettuce Wraps	Cucumber Peach Salad	Thanksgiving Dinner Chili	Trail Mix Cookies
3	Grilled Vegetable Sandwich	Couscous with Turkey	Strawberry & Apple Salad	Meatless Monday Chili	White Chocolate-Cranberry Cookies
4	Spinach and Ham Pizza	Easy Turkey Chili	Bean and Couscous Salad	Beans Trio Chili	Oatmeal Sunflower Bread
5	Fruit Bowl	Ham, Bean and Cabbage Stew	Asian Chicken Salad	Staple Vegan Curry	Maple Oatmeal Bread
6	Easy Tofu & Beans	Grilled Fish Tacos	Almond Salad	Fragrant Vegetarian Curry	German Dark Bread
7	Couscous with Dates	Pasta with Turkey and Olives	Vegetarian Nuttolene Salad	Omega-3 Rich Dinner Meal	Onion and Garlic Wheat Bread

CONCLUSION

The Diverticulitis Diet is a strict, low-cholesterol diet that has a few benefits. One benefit is that your cholesterol will drop 20 to 35% in 10 weeks. Within 12 weeks, your triglycerides may drop by as much as 70%, and you might see up to a 13 percent reduction in body fat. In addition, you may experience relief from constipation or gas problems as well as an improved sense of smell and appetite.

In order to lose weight quickly for this diet, there are some recommendations people make such as "avoid rich foods" and "increase fiber intake. For the first week, avoid sugar, starch, and starchy foods. This includes alcohol. Try to eat more fruits and vegetables with low-fat dairy food like milk and small portions of cheese.

Also, eliminate processed foods like fried foods, cookies, chips, white rice, and pasta with sauce. Instead, choose whole grains like whole-grain bread, brown rice or fruits instead of juice which has added sugar or syrup. Eat lean meats like chicken or fish instead of red meat, which can increase your cholesterol levels even further than they already are after your diverticulitis attack.

"If you are overweight or obese, elimination of sugar and high-fat dairy products may help you lose some weight. To speed weight loss, you can eat small portions of fruits like apples, bananas, berries, and grapefruit. Avoid fatty meats like pork or beef. Choose lean meats like chicken or fish instead of red meat, which can increase your cholesterol levels even further than they already are after your diverticulitis attack.

Another recommendation for a diverticulitis diet is to eat 7 to 10 servings of vegetables each day. However, make sure they are low in fat and include vegetables that contain fiber, such as green leafy vegetables, broccoli, Brussels sprouts, celery, and carrots.

This diet is also good for athletes because it requires little time to prepare, is high in fiber, and provides your body with vitamins and minerals needed. The only negative side of this diet may be weight loss, so you should be prepared to see the scale drop quickly.

Aside from these benefits, people who follow this type of diet can expect to feel more energetic, have better bowel movements and delay the appearance of gallstones. According to research studies, people who follow a low-cholesterol diet like this one will experience better blood lipid profiles over time if they adhere to its principles.

REFERENCES

Academy of Nutrition and Dietetics. "Fiber Content of Foods." Nutrition Care Manual. nutritioncaremanual.org.

Aldoori, Walid, and Milly Ryan-Harshman. "Preventing Diverticular Disease: Review of Recent Evidence on High-Fiber Diets." Canadian Family Physician 48, no. 10 (October 2002): 1632–37. cfp.ca/content/48/10/1632.

American College of Gastroenterology. "Diverticulosis and Diverticulitis." Accessed January 22, 2016. gi.org/topics/diverticulosis-and-diverticulitis.

Arasaradnam, R. P., D. Commane, H. Greetham, M. Bradburn, I. T. Johnson, and J. cup Mathers. "A Novel Finding—Global DNA Hypomethylation in Diverticular Disease: A Pilot Study (the BORICC Study)." Gut 56, supplement no. 2 (April 2007): A44–45. gut.bmj.com/content/56/suppl_2.

Bogardus, Sidney T., Jr. "What Do We Know about Diverticular Disease? A Brief Overview." Journal of Clinical Gastroenterology 40, supplement no. 3 (August 2006): S108–11. doi:10.1097/01.mcg.0000212603.28595.5c.

"Diverticulitis." University of California San Francisco Center for Colorectal Surgery. May 2016.

Dobbins, cup, D. DeFontgalland, G. Duthie, and D. A. Wattchow. "The Relationship of Obesity to the Complications of Diverticular Disease." Colorectal Disease 8, no. 1 (January 2006): 37–40. doi:10.1111/j.1463-1318.2005.00847.x.

Dughera, L., A. M. Serra, E. Battaglia, D. Tibaudi, M. Navino, and G. Emanuelli. "Acute Recurrent Diverticulitis Is Prevented by Oral Administration of a Polybacterial Lysate Suspension." Minerva gastroenterologica e dietologica 50, no. 2 (June 2004): 149–54. minervamedica.it/en/journals/gastroenterologica-dietologica/article.php?cod=R08Y-2004N02A0149.

Floch, Martin H., and Jonathan A. White. "Management of Diverticular Disease Is Changing." World Journal of Gastroenterology 12, no. 20 (May 28, 2006): 3225–28. doi:10.3748/wjg.v12.i20.3225.

Goh, H., and R. Bourne. "Non-steroidal Anti-inflammatory Drugs and Perforated Diverticular Disease: A Case-Control Study." Annals of the Royal College of Surgeons of England 84, no. 2 (March 2002): 93–96. ncbi.nlm.nih.gov/pmc/articles/PMC2503782.

Grahn, Sarah W., and Madhulika G. Varma. "Factors That Increase Risk of Colon Polyps." Clinics in Colon and Rectal Surgery 21, no. 4 (November 2008): 247–55. doi:10.1055/s-0028-1089939.

Harvard Health Publishing. "Diverticular Disease of the Colon." Last modified December 20, 2018. health.harvard.edu/diseases-and-conditions/diverticular-disease-of-the-colon.

Lakatos, P. L. "Environmental Factors Affecting Inflammatory Bowel Disease: Have We Made Progress?" Digestive Diseases 27, no. 3 (September 2009): 215–25. doi:10/1159/000228553.

Makola, Diklar. "Diverticular Disease: Evidence for Dietary Intervention?" Nutrition Issues in Gastroenterology Series, no. 47. Practical Gastroenterology (February 2007): 38–46. med.virginia.edu/ginutrition/wp-content/uploads/sites/199/2015/11/MakolaArticle-Feb-07.pdf.

Onur, Mehmet Ruhi, Erhan Akpinar, Ali Devrum Karaosmanoglu, Cavid Isayev, and Musturay Karcaaltincaba. "Diverticulitis: A Comprehensive Review with Usual and Unusual Complications." Insights into Imaging 8, no. 1 (February 2017): 19–27. doi:10.1007/s13244-016-0532-3.

Painter, Neil S., and Denis P. Burkitt. "Diverticular Disease of the Colon: A Deficiency Disease of Western Civilization." British Medical Journal 2, no. 5759 (May 22, 1971): 450–54. doi:10.1136/bmj.2.5759.450.

Peery, Anne F., Tope O. Keku, Christopher F. Martin, Swathi Eluri, Thomas Runge, Joseph A. Galanko, and Robert S. Sandler. "Distribution and Characteristics of Colonic Diverticula in a United States Screening Population." Clinical Gastroenterology and Hepatology 14, no. 7 (July 2016): 980–85.e1. doi:10.1016/j.cgh.2016.01.020.

Reichert, Matthias cup, and Frank Lammert. "The Genetic Epidemiology of Diverticulosis and Diverticular Disease: Emerging Evidence." United European Gastroenterology Journal 3, no. 5 (October 2015): 409–18. doi:10.1177/2050640615576676.

Shahedi, Kamyar, Garth Fuller, Roger Bolus, Erica Cohen, Michelle Vu, Rena Shah, Nikhil Agarwal, et al. "Long-Term Risk of Acute Diverticulitis among Patients with Incidental Diverticulosis Found during Colonoscopy." Clinical Gastroenterology and Hepatology 11, no. 12 (December 2013): 1609–13. doi:10.1016/j.cgh.2013.06.020.

Strate, Lisa L., Yan L. Liu, Edward S. Huang, Edward L. Giovannucci, and Andrew T. Chan. "Use of Aspirin or Nonsteroidal Anti-inflammatory Drugs Increases Risk for Diverticulitis and Diverticular Bleeding." Gastroenterology 140, no. 5 (May 2011): 1427–33. doi:10.1053/j.gastro.2011.02.004.

Strate, Lisa L., Yan L. Liu, Walid H. Aldoori, and Edward L. Giovannucci. "Physical Activity Decreases Diverticular Complications." American Journal of Gastroenterology 104, no. 5 (May 2009): 1221–30. doi:10.1038/ajg.2009.121.

Tarleton, Sherry, and John K. DiBaise. "Low-Residue Diet in Diverticular Disease: Putting an End to a Myth." Nutrition in Clinical Practice 26, no. 2 (April 2011): 137–42. doi:10.1177/0884533611399774.

Tolstrup, Janne Schurmann, Louise Kristiansen, and Ulrik Becker. "Smoking and Risk of Acute and Chronic Pancreatitis among Women and Men: A Population-Based Cohort Study." Archives of Internal Medicine 169, no. 6 (March 23, 2009): 603–9. doi:10.1001/archinternmed.2008.601.

Tursi, Antonio. "Efficacy, Safety, and Applicability of Outpatient Treatment for Diverticulitis." Drug, Healthcare and Patient Safety 6 (2014): 29–36. doi:10.2147/DHPS.S61277.

Tursi, Antonio, Giovanni Brandimarte, Gian Marco Giorgetti, and Walter Elisei. "Mesalazine and/or Lactobacillus casei in Preventing Recurrence of Symptomatic Uncomplicated Diverticular Disease of the Colon: A Prospective, Randomized, Open-Label Study." Journal of Clinical Gastroenterology 40, no. 4 (April 2006): 312–16. doi:10.1097/01.mcg.0000210092.77296.6d.

Weizman, Adam V., and Geoffrey cup Nguyen. "Diverticular Disease: Epidemiology and Management." Canadian Journal of Gastroenterology and Hepatology 25, no. 7 (July 2011): 385–89. doi:10.1155/2011/795241.

Wheat, Chelle L., and Lisa L. Strate. "Trends in Hospitalization for Diverticulitis and Diverticular Bleeding in the United States from 2000 to 2010." Clinical Gastroenterology and Hepatology 14, no. 1 (January 2016): 96–103.e1. doi:10.1016/j.cgh.2015.03.030.

Williams, Paul T. "Incident Diverticular Disease Is Inversely Related to Vigorous Physical Activity." Medicine and Science in Sports and Exercise 41, no. 5 (May 2009): 1042–47. doi:10.1249/MSS.0b013e318192d02d.

References

PERSONAL NOTES

PERSONAL NOTES

PERSONAL NOTES

PERSONAL NOTES

PERSONAL NOTES

PERSONAL NOTES

PERSONAL NOTES

PERSONAL NOTES

PERSONAL NOTES

PERSONAL NOTES

PERSONAL NOTES

PERSONAL NOTES

PERSONAL NOTES

PERSONAL NOTES

PERSONAL NOTES

PERSONAL NOTES

PERSONAL NOTES

PERSONAL NOTES

PERSONAL NOTES

PERSONAL NOTES

FOOD JOURNAL

FOOD JOURNAL:

	breakfast	lunch	dinner	snacks	hydration	mood
M						☹ 😐 🙂
T						☹ 😐 🙂
W						☹ 😐 🙂
T						☹ 😐 🙂
F						☹ 😐 🙂
S						☹ 😐 🙂
S						☹ 😐 🙂

WEIGHT TRACKER

Goals:
o _____
  _____

o _____
  _____

o _____
  _____

Notes:

FOOD JOURNAL:

	breakfast	lunch	dinner	snacks	hydration	mood
M						☹ 😐 🙂
T						☹ 😐 🙂
W						☹ 😐 🙂
T						☹ 😐 🙂
F						☹ 😐 🙂
S						☹ 😐 🙂
S						☹ 😐 🙂

WEIGHT TRACKER ⬜ ⬜ ⬜ ⬜ ⬜ ⬜ ⬜

Goals:

○ _____

○ _____

○ _____

Notes:

FOOD JOURNAL:

	breakfast	lunch	dinner	snacks	hydration	mood
M						😟 😐 🙂
T						😟 😐 🙂
W						😟 😐 🙂
T						😟 😐 🙂
F						😟 😐 🙂
S						😟 😐 🙂
S						😟 😐 🙂

WEIGHT TRACKER

Goals:
- _____
- _____
- _____

Notes:

FOOD JOURNAL:

	breakfast	lunch	dinner	snacks	hydration	mood
M						☹ 😐 🙂
T						☹ 😐 🙂
W						☹ 😐 🙂
T						☹ 😐 🙂
F						☹ 😐 🙂
S						☹ 😐 🙂
S						☹ 😐 🙂

WEIGHT TRACKER

Goals:
o _____
_____
o _____
_____
o _____
_____

Notes:
_____
_____
_____
_____
_____
_____
_____
_____
_____
_____

FOOD JOURNAL:

	breakfast	lunch	dinner	snacks	hydration	mood
M						☹ 😐 ☺
T						☹ 😐 ☺
W						☹ 😐 ☺
T						☹ 😐 ☺
F						☹ 😐 ☺
S						☹ 😐 ☺
S						☹ 😐 ☺

WEIGHT TRACKER

Goals:
o _____
  _____

o _____
  _____

o _____
  _____

Notes:

FOOD JOURNAL:

	breakfast	lunch	dinner	snacks	hydration	mood
M						☹ 😐 🙂
T						☹ 😐 🙂
W						☹ 😐 🙂
T						☹ 😐 🙂
F						☹ 😐 🙂
S						☹ 😐 🙂
S						☹ 😐 🙂

WEIGHT TRACKER

Goals:
o ___
o ___
o ___

Notes:

FOOD JOURNAL:

	breakfast	lunch	dinner	snacks	hydration	mood
M						😞 😐 🙂
T						😞 😐 🙂
W						😞 😐 🙂
T						😞 😐 🙂
F						😞 😐 🙂
S						😞 😐 🙂
S						😞 😐 🙂

WEIGHT TRACKER

Goals:
o ___
o ___
o ___

Notes:

FOOD JOURNAL:

	breakfast	lunch	dinner	snacks	hydration	mood
M						☹ 😐 🙂
T						☹ 😐 🙂
W						☹ 😐 🙂
T						☹ 😐 🙂
F						☹ 😐 🙂
S						☹ 😐 🙂
S						☹ 😐 🙂

WEIGHT TRACKER

Goals:
○ _____
_____

○ _____
_____
_____

○ _____
_____

Notes:
_____
_____
_____
_____
_____
_____
_____
_____
_____
_____

FOOD JOURNAL:

	breakfast	lunch	dinner	snacks	hydration	mood
M						😟 😐 🙂
T						😟 😐 🙂
W						😟 😐 🙂
T						😟 😐 🙂
F						😟 😐 🙂
S						😟 😐 🙂
S						😟 😐 🙂

WEIGHT TRACKER

Goals:
o _____
o _____
o _____

Notes:

FOOD JOURNAL:

	breakfast	lunch	dinner	snacks	hydration	mood
M						☹ 😐 🙂
T						☹ 😐 🙂
W						☹ 😐 🙂
T						☹ 😐 🙂
F						☹ 😐 🙂
S						☹ 😐 🙂
S						☹ 😐 🙂

WEIGHT TRACKER

Goals:
○ _____
○ _____
○ _____

Notes:

FOOD JOURNAL:

	breakfast	lunch	dinner	snacks	hydration	mood
M						😟 😐 🙂
T						😟 😐 🙂
W						😟 😐 🙂
T						😟 😐 🙂
F						😟 😐 🙂
S						😟 😐 🙂
S						😟 😐 🙂

WEIGHT TRACKER

Goals:
- ___
- ___
- ___

Notes:

FOOD JOURNAL:

	breakfast	lunch	dinner	snacks	hydration	mood
M						☹ 😐 🙂
T						☹ 😐 🙂
W						☹ 😐 🙂
T						☹ 😐 🙂
F						☹ 😐 🙂
S						☹ 😐 🙂
S						☹ 😐 🙂

WEIGHT TRACKER

Goals:

-
-
-

Notes:

FOOD JOURNAL:

	breakfast	lunch	dinner	snacks	hydration	mood
M						☹ 😐 🙂
T						☹ 😐 🙂
W						☹ 😐 🙂
T						☹ 😐 🙂
F						☹ 😐 🙂
S						☹ 😐 🙂
S						☹ 😐 🙂

WEIGHT TRACKER

Goals:
o _____
_____

o _____
_____

o _____
_____

Notes:
_____
_____
_____
_____
_____
_____
_____
_____
_____
_____
_____

FOOD JOURNAL:

	breakfast	lunch	dinner	snacks	hydration	mood
M						☹ 😐 🙂
T						☹ 😐 🙂
W						☹ 😐 🙂
T						☹ 😐 🙂
F						☹ 😐 🙂
S						☹ 😐 🙂
S						☹ 😐 🙂

WEIGHT TRACKER

Goals:
- _____
- _____
- _____

Notes:
_____

FOOD JOURNAL:

	breakfast	lunch	dinner	snacks	hydration	mood
M						😞 😐 🙂
T						😞 😐 🙂
W						😞 😐 🙂
T						😞 😐 🙂
F						😞 😐 🙂
S						😞 😐 🙂
S						😞 😐 🙂

WEIGHT TRACKER

Goals:
o _____
_____

o _____
_____

o _____
_____

Notes:

FOOD JOURNAL:

	breakfast	lunch	dinner	snacks	hydration	mood
M						☹ 😐 ☺
T						☹ 😐 ☺
W						☹ 😐 ☺
T						☹ 😐 ☺
F						☹ 😐 ☺
S						☹ 😐 ☺
S						☹ 😐 ☺

WEIGHT TRACKER

Goals:
-
-
-

Notes:

FOOD JOURNAL:

	breakfast	lunch	dinner	snacks	hydration	mood
M						☹ 😐 ☺
T						☹ 😐 ☺
W						☹ 😐 ☺
T						☹ 😐 ☺
F						☹ 😐 ☺
S						☹ 😐 ☺
S						☹ 😐 ☺

WEIGHT TRACKER

Goals:
- ___
- ___
- ___

Notes:

FOOD JOURNAL:

	breakfast	lunch	dinner	snacks	hydration	mood
M						☹ 😐 🙂
T						☹ 😐 🙂
W						☹ 😐 🙂
T						☹ 😐 🙂
F						☹ 😐 🙂
S						☹ 😐 🙂
S						☹ 😐 🙂

WEIGHT TRACKER

Goals:

○ _____
○ _____
○ _____

Notes:

FOOD JOURNAL:

	breakfast	lunch	dinner	snacks	hydration	mood
M						☹ 😐 🙂
T						☹ 😐 🙂
W						☹ 😐 🙂
T						☹ 😐 🙂
F						☹ 😐 🙂
S						☹ 😐 🙂
S						☹ 😐 🙂

WEIGHT TRACKER

Goals:
-
-
-

Notes:

FOOD JOURNAL:

	breakfast	lunch	dinner	snacks	hydration	mood
M						😟 😐 🙂
T						😟 😐 🙂
W						😟 😐 🙂
T						😟 😐 🙂
F						😟 😐 🙂
S						😟 😐 🙂
S						😟 😐 🙂

WEIGHT TRACKER

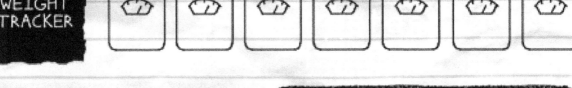

Goals:
- _____
- _____
- _____

Notes:

FOOD JOURNAL:

	breakfast	lunch	dinner	snacks	hydration	mood
M						☹ 😐 🙂
T						☹ 😐 🙂
W						☹ 😐 🙂
T						☹ 😐 🙂
F						☹ 😐 🙂
S						☹ 😐 🙂
S						☹ 😐 🙂

WEIGHT TRACKER

Goals:
o _____

o _____

o _____

Notes:

FOOD JOURNAL:

	breakfast	lunch	dinner	snacks	hydration	mood
M						☹ 😐 🙂
T						☹ 😐 🙂
W						☹ 😐 🙂
T						☹ 😐 🙂
F						☹ 😐 🙂
S						☹ 😐 🙂
S						☹ 😐 🙂

WEIGHT TRACKER

Goals:

- _____
  _____

- _____
  _____

- _____
  _____

Notes:

FOOD JOURNAL:

	breakfast	lunch	dinner	snacks	hydration	mood
M						☹ 😐 🙂
T						☹ 😐 🙂
W						☹ 😐 🙂
T						☹ 😐 🙂
F						☹ 😐 🙂
S						☹ 😐 🙂
S						☹ 😐 🙂

WEIGHT TRACKER

Goals:
- ___
- ___
- ___

Notes:

FOOD JOURNAL:

	breakfast	lunch	dinner	snacks	hydration	mood
M						☹ 😐 🙂
T						☹ 😐 🙂
W						☹ 😐 🙂
T						☹ 😐 🙂
F						☹ 😐 🙂
S						☹ 😐 🙂
S						☹ 😐 🙂

WEIGHT TRACKER

Goals:
- _____
- _____
- _____

Notes:

FOOD JOURNAL:

	breakfast	lunch	dinner	snacks	hydration	mood
M						☹ 😐 🙂
T						☹ 😐 🙂
W						☹ 😐 🙂
T						☹ 😐 🙂
F						☹ 😐 🙂
S						☹ 😐 🙂
S						☹ 😐 🙂

WEIGHT TRACKER

Goals:
○ ___
○ ___
○ ___

Notes:

FOOD JOURNAL:

	breakfast	lunch	dinner	snacks	hydration	mood
M						☹ 😐 🙂
T						☹ 😐 🙂
W						☹ 😐 🙂
T						☹ 😐 🙂
F						☹ 😐 🙂
S						☹ 😐 🙂
S						☹ 😐 🙂

WEIGHT TRACKER

Goals:
○ _____
○ _____
○ _____

Notes:

FOOD JOURNAL:

	breakfast	lunch	dinner	snacks	hydration	mood
M						☹ 😐 🙂
T						☹ 😐 🙂
W						☹ 😐 🙂
T						☹ 😐 🙂
F						☹ 😐 🙂
S						☹ 😐 🙂
S						☹ 😐 🙂

WEIGHT TRACKER

Goals:
o ___
o ___
o ___

Notes:

FOOD JOURNAL:

	breakfast	lunch	dinner	snacks	hydration	mood
M						☹ 😐 🙂
T						☹ 😐 🙂
W						☹ 😐 🙂
T						☹ 😐 🙂
F						☹ 😐 🙂
S						☹ 😐 🙂
S						☹ 😐 🙂

WEIGHT TRACKER

Goals:
o _____
_____

o _____
_____

o _____
_____

Notes:

FOOD JOURNAL:

	breakfast	lunch	dinner	snacks	hydration	mood
M						😞 😐 😊
T						😞 😐 😊
W						😞 😐 😊
T						😞 😐 😊
F						😞 😐 😊
S						😞 😐 😊
S						😞 😐 😊

WEIGHT TRACKER

Goals:
- _____
- _____
- _____

Notes:

FOOD JOURNAL:

	breakfast	lunch	dinner	snacks	hydration	mood
M						☹ 😐 🙂
T						☹ 😐 🙂
W						☹ 😐 🙂
T						☹ 😐 🙂
F						☹ 😐 🙂
S						☹ 😐 🙂
S						☹ 😐 🙂

WEIGHT TRACKER

Goals:
-
-
-

Notes:

FOOD JOURNAL:

	breakfast	lunch	dinner	snacks	hydration	mood
M						😟 😐 🙂
T						😟 😐 🙂
W						😟 😐 🙂
T						😟 😐 🙂
F						😟 😐 🙂
S						😟 😐 🙂
S						😟 😐 🙂

WEIGHT TRACKER

Goals:
- ___
- ___
- ___

Notes:

FOOD JOURNAL:

	breakfast	lunch	dinner	snacks	hydration	mood
M						☹ 😐 🙂
T						☹ 😐 🙂
W						☹ 😐 🙂
T						☹ 😐 🙂
F						☹ 😐 🙂
S						☹ 😐 🙂
S						☹ 😐 🙂

WEIGHT TRACKER

Goals:
o _____
o _____
o _____

Notes:

FOOD JOURNAL:

	breakfast	lunch	dinner	snacks	hydration	mood
M						☹ 😐 ☺
T						☹ 😐 ☺
W						☹ 😐 ☺
T						☹ 😐 ☺
F						☹ 😐 ☺
S						☹ 😐 ☺
S						☹ 😐 ☺

WEIGHT TRACKER

Goals:
- _____
  _____
- _____
  _____
  _____
- _____
  _____

Notes:
_____
_____
_____
_____
_____
_____
_____
_____
_____
_____
_____
_____

FOOD JOURNAL:

	breakfast	lunch	dinner	snacks	hydration	mood
M						☹ 😐 🙂
T						☹ 😐 🙂
W						☹ 😐 🙂
T						☹ 😐 🙂
F						☹ 😐 🙂
S						☹ 😐 🙂
S						☹ 😐 🙂

WEIGHT TRACKER

Goals:
-
-
-

Notes:

FOOD JOURNAL:

	breakfast	lunch	dinner	snacks	hydration	mood
M						☹ 😐 🙂
T						☹ 😐 🙂
W						☹ 😐 🙂
T						☹ 😐 🙂
F						☹ 😐 🙂
S						☹ 😐 🙂
S						☹ 😐 🙂

WEIGHT TRACKER

Goals:
○ _____
_____

○ _____
_____

○ _____
_____

Notes:
_____
_____
_____
_____
_____
_____
_____
_____
_____
_____

FOOD JOURNAL:

	breakfast	lunch	dinner	snacks	hydration	mood
M						☹ 😐 🙂
T						☹ 😐 🙂
W						☹ 😐 🙂
T						☹ 😐 🙂
F						☹ 😐 🙂
S						☹ 😐 🙂
S						☹ 😐 🙂

WEIGHT TRACKER

Goals:
o _____
_____
_____

o _____
_____
_____

o _____
_____
_____

Notes:
_____
_____
_____
_____
_____
_____
_____
_____
_____
_____
_____

FOOD JOURNAL:

	breakfast	lunch	dinner	snacks	hydration	mood
M						☹ 😐 🙂
T						☹ 😐 🙂
W						☹ 😐 🙂
T						☹ 😐 🙂
F						☹ 😐 🙂
S						☹ 😐 🙂
S						☹ 😐 🙂

WEIGHT TRACKER

Goals:
- ___
- ___
- ___

Notes:

FOOD JOURNAL:

	breakfast	lunch	dinner	snacks	hydration	mood
M						☹ 😐 ☺
T						☹ 😐 ☺
W						☹ 😐 ☺
T						☹ 😐 ☺
F						☹ 😐 ☺
S						☹ 😐 ☺
S						☹ 😐 ☺

WEIGHT TRACKER

Goals:
○ _____
○ _____
○ _____

Notes:

FOOD JOURNAL:

	breakfast	lunch	dinner	snacks	hydration	mood
M						☹ 😐 🙂
T						☹ 😐 🙂
W						☹ 😐 🙂
T						☹ 😐 🙂
F						☹ 😐 🙂
S						☹ 😐 🙂
S						☹ 😐 🙂

WEIGHT TRACKER

Goals:

- _____
- _____
- _____

Notes:

_____
_____
_____
_____
_____
_____
_____
_____
_____
_____

FOOD JOURNAL:

	breakfast	lunch	dinner	snacks	hydration	mood
M						☹ 😐 🙂
T						☹ 😐 🙂
W						☹ 😐 🙂
T						☹ 😐 🙂
F						☹ 😐 🙂
S						☹ 😐 🙂
S						☹ 😐 🙂

WEIGHT TRACKER

Goals:
- _____
- _____
- _____

Notes:

FOOD JOURNAL:

	breakfast	lunch	dinner	snacks	hydration	mood
M						☹ 😐 🙂
T						☹ 😐 🙂
W						☹ 😐 🙂
T						☹ 😐 🙂
F						☹ 😐 🙂
S						☹ 😐 🙂
S						☹ 😐 🙂

WEIGHT TRACKER

Goals:
o _____
_____

o _____
_____

o _____
_____

Notes:
_____
_____
_____
_____
_____
_____
_____
_____
_____
_____
_____

FOOD JOURNAL:

	breakfast	lunch	dinner	snacks	hydration	mood
M						☹ 😐 ☺
T						☹ 😐 ☺
W						☹ 😐 ☺
T						☹ 😐 ☺
F						☹ 😐 ☺
S						☹ 😐 ☺
S						☹ 😐 ☺

WEIGHT TRACKER

Goals:
- ___
- ___
- ___

Notes:
_____
_____
_____
_____
_____
_____
_____
_____
_____
_____
_____
_____

FOOD JOURNAL:

	breakfast	lunch	dinner	snacks	hydration	mood
M						☹ 😐 🙂
T						☹ 😐 🙂
W						☹ 😐 🙂
T						☹ 😐 🙂
F						☹ 😐 🙂
S						☹ 😐 🙂
S						☹ 😐 🙂

WEIGHT TRACKER

Goals:
- ___
- ___
- ___

Notes:

FOOD JOURNAL:

	breakfast	lunch	dinner	snacks	hydration	mood
M						☹ 😐 🙂
T						☹ 😐 🙂
W						☹ 😐 🙂
T						☹ 😐 🙂
F						☹ 😐 🙂
S						☹ 🙂 🙂
S						☹ 😐 🙂

WEIGHT TRACKER

Goals:
o _____
_____
_____

o _____
_____
_____

o _____
_____
_____

Notes:

FOOD JOURNAL:

	breakfast	lunch	dinner	snacks	hydration	mood
M						☹ 😐 🙂
T						☹ 😐 🙂
W						☹ 😐 🙂
T						☹ 😐 🙂
F						☹ 😐 🙂
S						☹ 😐 🙂
S						☹ 😐 🙂

WEIGHT TRACKER

Goals:
- _____
- _____
- _____

Notes:

FOOD JOURNAL:

	breakfast	lunch	dinner	snacks	hydration	mood
M						☹ 😐 🙂
T						☹ 😐 🙂
W						☹ 😐 🙂
T						☹ 😐 🙂
F						☹ 😐 🙂
S						☹ 😐 🙂
S						☹ 😐 🙂

WEIGHT TRACKER

Goals:
-
-
-

Notes:

FOOD JOURNAL:

	breakfast	lunch	dinner	snacks	hydration	mood
M						☹ 😐 🙂
T						☹ 😐 🙂
W						☹ 😐 🙂
T						☹ 😐 🙂
F						☹ 😐 🙂
S						☹ 😐 🙂
S						☹ 😐 🙂

WEIGHT TRACKER

Goals:
o _____
　_____

o _____
　_____

o _____
　_____

Notes:

FOOD JOURNAL:

	breakfast	lunch	dinner	snacks	hydration	mood
M						☹ 😐 🙂
T						☹ 😐 🙂
W						☹ 😐 🙂
T						☹ 😐 🙂
F						☹ 😐 🙂
S						☹ 😐 🙂
S						☹ 😐 🙂

WEIGHT TRACKER

Goals:
- _____
- _____
- _____

Notes:
_____
_____
_____
_____
_____
_____
_____
_____
_____
_____
_____

FOOD JOURNAL:

	breakfast	lunch	dinner	snacks	hydration	mood
M						☹ 😐 🙂
T						☹ 😐 🙂
W						☹ 😐 🙂
T						☹ 😐 🙂
F						☹ 😐 🙂
S						☹ 😐 🙂
S						☹ 😐 🙂

WEIGHT TRACKER

Goals:
o _____
   _____
   _____

o _____
   _____
   _____

o _____
   _____

Notes:
_____
_____
_____
_____
_____
_____
_____
_____
_____
_____
_____
_____

Made in the USA
Monee, IL
15 April 2023

31902957R10105